My Turn

CARING FOR AGING PARENTS & OTHER ELDERLY LOVED ONES

A DAUGHTER'S PERSPECTIVE

SANDRA W. HAYMON, Ph.D.

MAGNOLIA
PRODUCTIONS

MAGNOLIA PRODUCTIONS, INC.
P.O. BOX 13705
TALLAHASSEE, FL 32317-3705
1-888-2OLD-AGE
(Toll Free: 1-888-265-3243)
Fax: 1-904-894-9676
E-Mail: shaymon@applicom.com
http://www.applicom.com/aging/

Cover Photos: The photo on the left is of Sandra Haymon and her mother, Mildred, when Sandra was little and it was her mother's turn to take care of Sandra. The photo on the right of Sandra and her mother shows that it is Sandra's turn to be the caregiver.

Haymon, Sandra W.
My Turn: Caring for Aging Parents &
Other Elderly Loved Ones / Sandra W. Haymon, Ph.D.

Magnolia Productions, Inc.
P.O. Box 13705
Tallahassee, Fl 32317-3705.

ISBN: 0-9652965-0-4
Printed in the United States of America
First Printing: August, 1996

ACKNOWLEDGEMENT

This publication is based on my personal story of caring for my aging mother and stepfather. I want to thank everyone who assisted and supported me during the process of taking care of my folks. I especially want to thank all of my guardian angels, who not only protected me, but lighted my path and showed me the way down an unfamiliar road marked with many obstacles. I want to thank my two best friends, Patty Rubino-Brunetti and Darby Godwin, Ph.D., who were always there to listen, to let me vent, to allow me to cry, to help me see the humor, and to encourage me. I'm not sure I would have made it without you. A very special thank you to my sister, Wanda, who came every time I called her. I want to thank Steven C. Ruby for his ongoing support and technical guidance. I also want to thank Gary W. Peterson, Ph.D., for his editorial comments and counsel and for being my mentor for nearly a decade. Vera Gadman deserves special thanks for her guidance and creativity. I must also thank Kathryn Childers for lending her many years of experience in television to the interview process. Thanks to Mary Hoekstra for her meticulous proofreading. Cresyl, Amy, and Hippie remained loyal and constant companions and I thank them. There are many others who graciously gave their time and energy because they believed this to be a worthwhile project. Thank you all for helping to make this possible.

Sandra,

Spring, 1996

For those who are taking "their turn."

AUTHOR'S NOTE

There is great value in staying in touch with your own internal feelings. Sometimes, even in the face of much information to the contrary, our own heartfelt feelings tell us to do the opposite of what our brain is telling us. I encourage you to pay attention to those feelings. All too often, we are inundated with so much information that we seem paralyzed as to what to do. Then, unfortunately, we start looking outside ourselves for answers and maybe even for someone else to make our decisions for us. One of the ways I identify when I am in this position is to note my own confusion. When I feel confused, it is helpful for me to find a place where I can be still and quiet. Then I listen to my own inner voice.

We are all gifted with a wonderful internal mechanism that will guide us along the path toward our highest good. When we make choices that are in our highest good, it contributes to the highest good of others and to the universe, as well. So trust yourself! When you feel torn between what you feel and what you think, take a moment to get in touch with what you really feel, then trust that feeling.

The process of caring for an aging relative, in itself, is absolutely neutral. You may choose to experience your turn as difficult and unpleasant, or as positive, meaningful, and adding value to your life. It is your choice! As I reflect on these past few years, I think of Charles Dickens' words in <u>A Tale of Two Cities</u>, "It was the best of times, it was the worst of times..." Having the opportunity to provide care for my own parents has truly been, and continues to be, a rewarding learning experience in my own growth process. It has enabled me to examine my own values, as well as to come to terms with my own mortality. My emotions have run the full gamut. My heart goes out to each and every one of you and I sincerely wish you the very best as you take your turn.

Sandra,

Spring, 1996

TABLE OF CONTENTS

CHAPTER 1
Learn how caring for elderly family members was handled in the past;
how this is presently being handled; and speculations about how this may be
handled in the future.

CHAPTER 2
Confront your myths and denial about your parents' ability to safely live
alone. Use the enclosed "Red Flag Checklist."

CHAPTER 3
Make difficult choices in advance. Hospitalization, CPR, feeding tubes, all have
pros and cons. They may prolong life, but could prolong the dying process.

CHAPTER 4
Legal documents – Do Not Hospitalize; No CPR; Living Wills; Health Care
Surrogate; Health Care Proxy; Durable Power of Attorney; Guardianship;
and other directives are explained in clear, easy to understand language.
Use enclosed legal forms to ensure your wishes are specified.

CHAPTER 5
Know your loved ones' needs and level of functioning. Consider various
care options – home assistance, adult day care, congregate community living,
nursing homes, Alzheimer's units. Be confident in your choice of care.

CHAPTER 6
Decode the "alphabet soup" used by medical and legal professionals. Know
what SS; SSI; OSS; HMOs; VA; and other acronyms mean to you. Understand
Medicare Parts A and B, Medicaid, Supplemental Security Income, Optional
Supplemental Income, Veteran's Benefits, reverse mortgages, and more.

FEELINGS CHECKLIST

Before you turn to the next page, or listen to these tapes, please take a moment to check every feeling you have had regarding caring for your aging loved one.

☐ Frustrated	☐ Guilty	☐ Angry	☐ Privileged	☐ Sad
☐ Assertive	☐ Overwhelmed	☐ Compassionate	☐ Powerless	☐ Out-of-Control
☐ Loving	☐ Forgiving	☐ Depressed	☐ Immobilized	☐ Misunderstood
☐ Appreciated	☐ Unappreciated	☐ Happy	☐ Relieved	☐ Burdened
☐ Resentful	☐ Used	☐ Abused	☐ Useful	☐ Helpless
☐ Hopeless	☐ Scared	☐ Afraid	☐ Understood	☐ Glad
☐ Sick	☐ Powerful	☐ Enraged	☐ Grateful	☐ Empowered
☐ Strong	☐ Weak	☐ Hurt	☐ Stressed	☐ Disappointed
☐ Fearful	☐ Alone	☐ Stupid	☐ Unprepared	☐ Demoralized
☐ Positive	☐ Negative	☐ Tired	☐ Rested	☐ Peaceful
☐ Agitated	☐ Centered	☐ Energized	☐ Unsuccessful	☐ Successful
☐ Fatigued	☐ Defeated	☐ Intolerant	☐ Tolerant	☐ Aggressive
☐ Agonized	☐ Curious	☐ Anxious	☐ Apologetic	☐ Indifferent
☐ Arrogant	☐ Confident	☐ Determined	☐ Envious	☐ Exasperated
☐ Horrified	☐ Warm	☐ Jealous	☐ Disbelieving	☐ Disgusted
☐ Sarcastic	☐ Paranoid	☐ Perplexed	☐ Satisfied	☐ Dissatisfied
☐ Indecisive	☐ Shocked	☐ Suspicious	☐ Sympathetic	☐ Regretful
☐ Meditative	☐ Spiritual	☐ Indifferent	☐ Withdrawn	☐ Blissful
☐ Smart	☐ Naive	☐ Joyful	☐ Thankful	☐ Alienated
☐ Annoyed	☐ Apathetic	☐ Discouraged	☐ Confused	☐ Frightened
☐ Confident	☐ Excited	☐ Exhausted	☐ Enthusiastic	☐ Hostile
☐ Humiliated	☐ Hysterical	☐ Loved	☐ Miserable	☐ Optimistic
☐ Proud	☐ Puzzled	☐ Remorseful	☐ Stubborn	☐ Surprised
☐ Omnipotent	☐ Resented	☐ Lonely	☐ Tired	☐ Bored

RED FLAG CHECKLIST

Early Warning Signs: Any one of these may indicate a decreased ability on the part of your loved one to safely function on her or his own.

Decreased Cognitive Functioning:

☐ General confusion

☐ Gets lost in own neighborhood

☐ Can't remember names of family members

☐ Short-term memory loss

☐ Forgets and leaves the car/truck running

☐ Confuses the heat thermostat with the air-conditioning

☐ Wears more than one outfit at the same time (several shirts/blouses; pants/dresses)

☐ Forgets to feed pets or clean cat litter pans

☐ Forgets to retrieve mail from mailbox for several days

☐ Does not remember eating meals

☐ Forgets appointments frequently

☐ Leaves house keys hanging on the outside of doors

☐ Calls police frequently for unapparent reasons

☐ Doesn't know who the President of the U.S. is

☐ Inability to count backwards from 20

☐ Cannot remember/recite the alphabet

Decreased Physical Functioning:

☐ Lacks coordination (stumbles/falls)

☐ Bladder/bowel incontinent (soils underclothes)

☐ No longer able to shave himself

☐ Inability to hear phone/doorbell

☐ Stays in bed even when not sick

☐ Requires help getting out of bed/chairs

☐ Unusual shakiness of hands and/or legs

☐ Unexplained bruises/injuries (check out possibilities of physical abuse, especially if bruises/injuries occur on upper body or face)

☐ Night sweats

☐ Frequent diarrhea

☐ Seeing several physicians for the same complaints

☐ Difficulty using a telephone

☐ Difficulty operating television set

☐ No longer able to operate washing machine/dryer properly

Decreased General Functioning:

☐ Overly suspicious (inappropriately questions the motives of others)

☐ Paranoid behaviors (bars doors/windows; looks under beds and in closets without reason)

☐ Misplaces things and accuses others of stealing them

☐ Becomes upset easily (cries/laughs inappropriately)

☐ Appears more depressed than usual

☐ Appears depressed more frequently

☐ Often appears sad/depressed

☐ Becomes extremely afraid of animals

☐ Becomes obsessed with a pet or treats pet as having human qualities

☐ Social withdrawal

☐ Isolation/estrangement

☐ Appears unusually anxious

☐ Accidental hypo- or hyper-thermia (exposure to extreme temperatures—hot or cold)

☐ Outbursts of anger/aggression

☐ Extremely restless/fidgety

☐ Frequently goes to bed/sleep one to two hours earlier than usual at night

☐ Nighttime sleep is accompanied with several, brief awakenings

☐ Nightmares

☐ Insomnia

☐ Frequent use of sleep aids

☐ Night prowls (cat naps during the day then wanders around the house during the night)

Decreased Social Functioning:

- ☐ Conflicts with neighbors
- ☐ Becomes hostile for unapparent reasons
- ☐ Diminished social skills
- ☐ Inability to carry on two-way communication

Decreased Eating Habits:

- ☐ Eats food that is not fresh
- ☐ Eats unbalanced meals (consuming lots of sweets)
- ☐ Hordes food
- ☐ Cooks food and forgets to eat it

Decreased Personal Hygiene/Cleanliness of Environment:

- ☐ Does not take regular baths or shampoo hair
- ☐ Fails to maintain a clean home environment
- ☐ Allows garbage to collect inside house

Disorientation:

- ☐ With respect to time: Doesn't know what time of day it is; what day of the week it is; what month it is; what season it is; or what year it is
- ☐ Doesn't know where she/he is physically
- ☐ Doesn't know what city/town/state she/he is in

Decreased Ability to Handle Money Matters:

- ☐ Hides/loses money and cannot remember where it is
- ☐ Carelessness in paying bills (paying bills more than once or not at all)
- ☐ Unintentional shoplifting (takes goods without realizing they're not paid for)
- ☐ Uncontrolled spending sprees
- ☐ Pays money to strangers for work that is not performed
- ☐ Gives money to strangers
- ☐ Careless with checks (signs blank check and gives to others)
- ☐ Puts new acquaintances on checking/savings accounts
- ☐ Withdraws money from the bank for strangers
- ☐ Easily manipulated by unscrupulous vendors/salespeople/telemarketers

CRITICAL RED FLAGS

Signs of potential for physical harm to self or others

- ☐ Chokes on food
- ☐ Leaves gas on with no flame
- ☐ Forgets pots cooking on the stove
- ☐ Burns food frequently
- ☐ Inability to take medications properly
- ☐ Inability to safely drive car/truck, yet continues to drive
- ☐ Cigarette burns on clothing/furniture
- ☐ Gets lost in own neighborhood
- ☐ Often loses balance/stumbles/falls frequently
- ☐ Carelessness with firearms

ALCOHOL SPECIFIC INDICATORS

Due to a change in physiology in elderly individuals, consumption of alcohol could lead to problems, even when the amount consumed is minimal. Even one daily cocktail, combined with some over-the-counter, as well as some prescribed medications, may be dangerous.

- ☐ Continues to drink in a social context
- ☐ Obvious intoxication
- ☐ Previous history of alcohol abuse
- ☐ Diagnosis of cirrhosis of the liver
- ☐ Previous arrests/tickets for DWI (driving while under the influence of alcohol)
- ☐ Accidents which were alcohol-related
- ☐ Previous hospitalizations for alcohol-related problems
- ☐ Hides alcohol
- ☐ The presence of lots of empty alcohol containers (beer cans; wine/liquor bottles)
- ☐ Frequent trips to neighborhood stores (for the purpose of buying beer/wine/liquor)
- ☐ Previous history of behavioral problems
- ☐ Previous history of psychiatric problems
- ☐ Impairments in the ability to process verbal information
- ☐ Drinking oneself into oblivion
- ☐ Passes out from alcohol
- ☐ Vomits in bed (This is extremely dangerous due to possibility of choking on vomit.)

Delirium tremens:

- ☐ Hears voices/sounds that are not there
- ☐ Sees things that are not there

It may be helpful to review this completed Red Flag Checklist with your loved one's physician and request further screening.

About the interviewer: Kathryn Childers has 15 years experience in television interviewing. She was the producer and host of her own daily talk show in Corpus Christi, Texas on KIII-TV, where she interviewed thousands of people, including such celebrities as Walter Cronkite; David Brinkley; First Ladies Rosalynn Carter and Barbara Bush; author James Mitchener; Hugh Downs; Nolan Ryan, Joan Lunden; and Charles Gibson. Her television chats included more than 100 major stars such as Robert Wagner; Lucille Ball; James Earl Jones; Dolly Parton; and Jamie Lee Curtis. Kathryn Childers' Specials aired in prime time featuring famous South Texas places and personalities. Kathryn was also elected to ABC Television Network's eight-member National Marketing Board, for which she attended quarterly, decision-making meetings in New York and Los Angeles.
In 1969, Kathryn was selected as one of our nation's first female Secret Service agents and was given the assignment of protecting, among others, John and Caroline Kennedy; Queen Sophia of Spain; First Lady Patricia Nixon and the Nixon daughters; Israeli Prime Minister Golda Meir; and Imelda Marcos.

INTRODUCTION

February 14, 1994 started as a typical day for Sandra Haymon. Her psychology residency was taking most of her time. A fifteen-hour day was not unusual. Booked with clients all day, she'd be lucky if she had time to run a mile after work. She'd hoped for three. Stacks of reading material littered her desk. A doctoral dissertation on work addiction had taken two years of research and she was ready for a break.

A note scribbled on her calendar reminded her to get a card for her stepfather and a box of candy for her mother. She'd drop them by after work. It was Valentine's Day. She always tried to do something nice on holidays. Like most Americans with elderly parents, Sandra wanted to believe her parents could still live alone. She did everything she could to maintain that myth.

She grew up in a tiny southern Alabama town, as the youngest of six children. Sandra Haymon despised her young life. Her abusive, alcoholic parents demanded hard work, but discouraged education. Book learning simply wasn't for girls. Daughters simply married and left home. When she was fifteen, Sandra met a local boy and did just that. In 1965, married girls weren't allowed in high school, so she found an adult-education center forty-five miles away. Sandra aced three years of course work in fourteen months. She'd hoped marriage would be her ticket out, but it was not. Sandra had swapped one abusive nightmare for another. She took courage and fled. Working full time while attending classes four nights a week, she graduated magna cum laude from Troy State University. A master's degree followed, and in 1992, Sandra Haymon earned a Ph.D. in Counseling Psychology and Human Systems from The Florida State University.

> Sandra wanted to believe her parents could still live alone.

Educated and independent, Sandra had grown beyond her childhood anger. Life was good — busy, but good. Then one emergency phone call changed everything. Carl, her stepfather, needed to be hospitalized and her mother had to be moved from their home. Overnight, her parents' independence shattered. She had known it was coming, but wasn't prepared for what followed. Sixteen moves and eighteen months later, her parents were finally safe and settled into an appropriate care facility. A year's research would follow for the answers she wished she'd had.

My Turn is a ready reference guide, intertwined with a heartfelt story shared by millions of Americans. Sandra says it was comedy and tragedy. There were good times and times that were not so good. Ironically, she says, she is closer to her parents now than ever before. She has learned more about forgiveness, compassion, and love than she ever thought possible.

OVERVIEW

Kathryn: Dr. Haymon, what do you mean when you say it is *your turn*?

Sandra: Let me share with you what happened to me and what's happening to millions of Americans every day. On Valentine's Day, 1994, I was 44 years old and had accomplished many of my life's goals. I had survived an abusive childhood. I had put myself through college. I'd gotten a private pilot's license. I'd run a marathon. I had earned a Ph.D. I thought there was nothing I couldn't handle. Yet on that day, I was presented with the greatest challenge of my life, the one for which I was least prepared. Within a 24-hour period, I had to decide what to do with my 80-year-old parents who could no longer take care of themselves.

K: I can't imagine that you would have been willing to take care of these people, considering how difficult your childhood was.

S: Growing up with alcoholic parents is horrible; there's no doubt about it. The last thing I wanted to do was to have to take care of them, but nobody else was willing to accept that responsibility. So I had to let go of my own anger and let go of my own pain. I realized I was taking care of them, not because of who they were, but because of who I was, and am. My definition of my role as a daughter had nothing to do with their definition of their role as my parents.

> ...we do have lots of choices — as long as we make those decisions in advance.

Whether you had a horrible childhood with abusive parents, and many of us did, or whether you had a great childhood with loving parents, the issues remain the same. Overnight I had to make major medical decisions for my stepfather, find a place where my mother could be cared for, move her from her home, and figure out how to pay for all of this. I was asked some of the most difficult questions I had ever been asked, and I didn't have the answers.

K: What were some of those questions?

S: Whether you're in an emergency room, or admitting your parents to a care facility, you will be asked about end-of-life medical decisions. For example, you will be asked whether they have a living will.

I want to take a minute here to mention something about living wills, because living wills tend to lull people into a false sense of security. Most living wills address only one issue, and that is whether the individual would want to be placed on artificial life support, such as feeding tubes or artificial respirators. And while it is important to make this decision, you also need to know there are many other decisions that need to be made, such as whether to administer CPR in the event of cardiac arrest or respiratory failure. I didn't know my folks had a choice, nor had I ever thought about why they might not want CPR. You might also be asked whether they have a Do Not Hospitalize Order. Again, I didn't know we had a choice. I had never considered the notion that we might not want to hospitalize them, that we might want to treat them at home or in a care facility. These are just some of the questions I was asked. Actually, we have many choices regarding medical decisions. The point I want to make is that we do have lots of choices, as long as we make those decisions in advance. However, we give up our choices when we don't plan ahead.

K: How can we plan ahead?

S: By discussing end-of-life choices with our elderly loved ones and insisting they make these decisions for themselves. We also need to ensure they complete the necessary forms so their wishes may be carried out. Another question I was asked was whether my folks had *advance directives*. I had no idea what an advance directive even was. I now know advance directives are legal documents which allow you to make your own medical decisions while you're competent to make them. And there are many advance directives — Living Wills, Do Not Hospitalize, Do Not Resuscitate, Surrogate Caregiver, Durable-Power of Attorney, Guardianship, and others — which allow personal choices to be carried out. At this time, I only want to make you aware these documents exist, and to remind you that if your parents don't make decisions for themselves, chances are you will have to make these heart-wrenching decisions for them.

> She never threw anything away. She had saved every one of her old purses for the last fifty years, and she used those old purses as her filing cabinets!

K: Were there other ways you could have been prepared for that day when it became your turn?

S: Yes. If I knew then what I know now, not only would I have talked to my folks and insisted they make their own end-of-life medical decisions, I would have ensured that they had regular physical and mental evaluations. And I would have insisted that my stepfather receive treatment for his alcoholism. I would have also known more about their finances and insurance policies, but sometimes that's easier said than done.

In my mother's case, she had a unique filing system. My mother was a Southern lady who had come through the Depression. She understood recycling before we even had a name for it. She never threw anything away. She had saved every one of her old purses for the last fifty years, and she used those old purses as her filing cabinets! She had red purses and brown purses. Black purses and blue purses. She had big purses and little purses, fat purses and flat purses. She hid those old purses in the tops of closets, under the beds, and between the mattresses on the beds. And, in no particular order, my mother kept their insurance policies, burial policies, bank statements, and other important and unimportant documents in those old purses. She also kept every greeting card ever sent to her, and hid money in the envelopes of those cards. Then she hid the cards in those old purses. I believe my mother kept every piece of mail addressed to Occupant in those purses. So when it became my turn, and I had to come up with their birth certificates, marriage certificates, insurance policies, and other important documents, I had to go through every envelope in every purse. It took me a solid week, working nonstop. Now that was the bad news. The good news was, I found nearly $2,000 hidden in those old purses and in the toes of old shoes. So you know what? I bought them some new furniture to take to the care facility and a filing cabinet!

> ## A lifetime of savings can evaporate within a few months.

I would have also known more about Medicare and Medicaid and other government assistance. In hopes of helping others to not be as overwhelmed as I was, I have provided a clear summary of certain programs, what they pay for and what they don't pay for, and the eligibility requirements for each.

K: Many people are worried about how they will pay for this. Could you give us some idea of how much these facilities cost?

S: Elder care in our country is extremely expensive. Nursing home care ranges anywhere from $25,000 to $75,000 a year. A lifetime of savings can evaporate within a few months.

K: So how do people pay for it?

S: Some people spend their life's savings, and when that's gone, they depend on government programs. Some people depend on their children to pay. Some have supplemental insurance policies, and others depend solely on government programs.

K: Could you have seen this day coming?

S: You know, at some level I knew I would be the one to inherit the responsibility of taking care of my mother and stepfather. However, I pretended that day would never come. Yet there were lots of "red flags" that indicated the day had already arrived. I just ignored them.

K: Don't you think most people ignore the flags?

S: Yes, and here are some examples of red flags: Both my mother and stepfather fell on several occasions, and even though some of their falls resulted in broken bones, we attributed those falls to loose rugs, the light not being on, or any number of external reasons. They also seemed unable to remember things. My mother would leave pots burning on the stove. And on more than one occasion they got lost within blocks of their own house.

K: So why didn't you put your parents in a care facility earlier?

S: I've explored that question, both within myself and with others who waited until they were forced to do something. It seems some of the reasons many of us don't move our folks into care facilities earlier is because we're either in denial, we don't want to see them lose their independence, or maybe we don't want our own lives to change. And it just may be that we don't want to face our own mortality.

K: Can you tell me briefly what you mean by the term, "denial?"

S: Denial is when we stick our heads in the sand and pretend nothing has changed. We actually hide from reality. And while this might protect us from some emotional pain, it may also allow life-threatening situations to occur, not only for our elderly loved ones, but for other people, as well. For example, there were lots of warning signs which indicated my stepfather should not continue to drive. I just pretended it was okay. I didn't want to take away his independence by taking away his truck keys. Then one day he mistook the accelerator for the brake. He created a three-car accident in a shopping center parking lot. It was a miracle that nobody was killed.

> We actually hide from reality. And while this might protect us from some emotional pain, it may also allow life-threatening situations to occur.

K: Dr. Haymon, how do we avoid being in denial in a situation like this?

S: I've created a red flag check list which I hope will help others do a *reality check*. It's very important to pay attention to signs that tell us something is not quite right. If it looks like something is wrong with the picture, then probably something's wrong with the picture. Check out your suspicions. Ask other family members, friends, and neighbors how they see your parents. When abnormal things happen, jot those things down and date it. Then, when you take your parents for their medical or mental evaluation, take that list with you. Review it with their doctor. Get her or him to help you decide if there's reason to be concerned. By all means, don't ignore red flags which might indicate you need to get your parents evaluated by a geriatric psychiatrist, as well as by a medical doctor.

K: **When we realize our parents can no longer safely live alone and take care of themselves, what are our choices? To borrow your phrase, where should they go when they can't go home?**

S: You actually have many choices. You may decide to hire someone to come live with them in their own home. It's important that elderly people be allowed to stay in their homes as long as they can *safely* do so. *Safely* is the operative word here. You may decide to move them in with you. Or you may opt for an adult foster home. Other choices include adult day care, assisted living facilities, nursing homes, Alzheimer's units, and state hospitals. There are many options. But in order to make a good decision, you have to know your parents' true level of functioning. There are different facilities for different levels of care. Placing them in an inappropriate facility may result in a number of unnecessary moves. My situation is a good example. In just one year, I moved my stepfather ten times and my mother six times. This was partially because they were placed in a care facility that was inappropriate for them from the beginning.

K: **I had no idea there were so many options. How are you and your parents doing now?**

S: For the first time in a long time, we all have some sense of settlement. They are living together in an Alzheimer's unit in a wonderful facility in Florida. They feel safe and secure and loved. As for me, these last several years have been the best of times and they've been the worst of times. The old saying that one person's garbage is another person's treasure suggests the notion that we have a choice about how we experience life events. So it is with taking care of aging relatives. It's not inherently joyful, nor is it inherently burdensome. We are wonderfully free to choose how we experience it. I truly hope that what I share with you about my turn will help you and others have a much less difficult time when it becomes your turn.

CHAPTER 1

OUR TURN

K: Most of us realize it won't be long before it's *our turn*. In fact, many of us are dealing with this, even as we speak. It's an age-old problem. How did we get here and where do we go from here? Have things really changed that much?

S: You know, Kathryn, as we approach midlife, many of us find we no longer have to crusade for every cause that comes along, nor do we have to try to right every wrong that's occurred throughout the millennia. Most of us have spent the past few decades educating ourselves, raising children, and establishing ourselves in careers. And just when we thought we could relax and coast for awhile, we're asked to walk an unfamiliar road. We're given no maps, no landmarks, no directions. We're asked to accept responsibility for caring for our aging parents. How can this be? It seems only yesterday we argued with them for our independence. We rebelled against the power they held over us. We rallied against everything they stood for. We blamed them for the state of the world. We despised their self-discipline and vowed to live our lives freely. They had so many rules about everything. I don't know about your parents, but mine thought they knew the *right* way for me to go, to live, to be. Yet now, when I so desperately need their answers, they have none.

I find that most of us want to care for our parents in the *right* way. We just don't know what the *right* way is. And, Kathryn, there are about fifteen million of us facing this problem today. The irony is, many of us marched together. We protested together. We fought the Vietnam war together. We were so empowered by numbers. It didn't matter what it was; we were all in it together. But now, now I'm not comforted knowing there are millions in the same boat with me. My anxiety increases as I talk to friends and relatives who are in similar situations. They are as lost as I was. Talk about anxiety. Pick up the newspaper or watch the six-o'clock news and listen to our congressmen and representatives argue and become angry over the national problem of how to care for our elderly citizens. You know, when it becomes our turn, we don't have the luxury of waiting until the President and Congress decide how much money they'll budget for elder care. When an elderly person has a stroke or an accident, or simply crosses the line between independence and dependence, many decisions have to be made immediately. Somebody has to take action. And when that elderly person is your relative, chances are, you will be the one who will have to make those decisions.

The number of people over 65 years of age has tripled since 1900. Furthermore, in the early 1900's there were approximately 14 adult caregivers for every person over 65. Today, there are only 4 of us for every elderly person.

K: Who are those caregivers, Dr. Haymon?

S: Traditionally, the primary responsibility of caring for elderly people fell to women who did not work outside the home. Now, even women with jobs are still expected to assume this responsibility. More than 90% of caregivers for elderly people are still women who may, or may not, work outside the home, who may, or may not, have children still at home. Even when it is a son's lot to have this responsibility…

K: Let me guess, it becomes his wife's job.

S: You got it. He delegates that responsibility to his wife. The stark reality is, the decision of who will assume the primary responsibility of caring for aging relatives historically has been, and continues to be, one of default. And that default is to women. Here is something else that may not surprise you — it is customarily the youngest daughter.

K: So you're saying, Dr. Haymon, that the number of people over 65 has tripled since 1900, yet the number of people to take care of them has dropped from 14 to 4. How can that be?

S: Well, Kathryn, let's think back to 1900 and what our culture was like at that time. We were primarily an agrarian society. The majority of the people

> ## The number of people over 65 years of age has tripled since 1900.

farmed and they had large families. It was not uncommon to have 8,10, even 12 children in one family. Kids were needed to help out on the farm. During that time, it was not only understood, it was expected, that families would take care of Grandma and Grandpa. Like the Waltons. During that period in time, it was not uncommon for two, three, maybe even four generations to live on the same farm land — sometimes even in the same house. So there were lots of people of various ages to help take care of Grandma and Grandpa when they got old. During that period in time, growing old and dying were part of the process of living.

Then we moved from a basically agrarian society into an industrial society. Since many people did not have an automobile, they left the farms and moved into town so they could be closer to the factories and stores. However, many elderly people refused to leave their farm homes. Physical distance created emotional distance. Then World War II came along. Men went off to war and many women went into the factories. This was the first time in our history that a large number of women entered the paid work force. Then, when the men came back from the war, not every woman came home. Many of them stayed on the assembly lines and others went into service industries. The focus in our country during that time was on productivity and consumer goods. The government saw the need for women, as well as men, to stay in the work force. So *Uncle Sam* assumed responsibility of providing places where our aging relatives could live. For the first time in our history, we delegated the responsibility of taking care of aging loved ones to total strangers.

In some families there was the proverbial "old maid" daughter. Today we would probably refer to her as the "independent woman who chose not to get married." It was understood, if she would take care of Grandma and Grandpa, she would be given the old home place, or the china, or some other tangible perk when they died. That was true in my own family. My Aunt Katie, my mother's sister, remained faithful in taking care of my grandmother and grandfather until they both died. Even though my grandmother lived about 10 years longer than my grandfather, Aunt Katie never married as long as either of her parents was living. Those families who didn't have an Aunt Katie had little choice except to put Grandma in a nursing home. There was extreme stigma attached to that. Neighbors would whisper about how awful it was to put her in a home, but what else could they do? There were house payments, car payments, and T.V. payments to be made and children to be sent to college. Most families were dependent on two incomes. So they had little choice but to put Grandma in a nursing home. And I say Grandma because women normally outlive their husbands and people commonly refer to their own parents as Grandma or Grandpa, or Grandmother or Grandfather, because that's what they teach their own children to call them.

> Aunt Katie never married as long as either of her parents were living.

K: Do you remember, as a little girl, going to the nursing home with your mother to visit your grandmother?

S: Actually, Kathryn, I remember the very day when we placed Grandma in a nursing home. It was in 1954 and I was not quite five years old. Even though I didn't understand it at the time, I knew placing my grandmother in a nursing home was an embarrassment to our family. My mother and I would go to visit her almost every Sunday. Although she was my father's mother, my dad hardly ever went. I really looked forward to those visits. She had lived in our home since before I was born. Now she was in a nursing home. I missed her and really looked forward to taking flowers to her from my mother's garden and things I had drawn for her. Yet I knew my mother would cry every time we left. I saw that was true for a lot of families. Many would come to visit and their Grandmas would beg to go home with them. That would break their hearts. So many of them stopped visiting, except for birthdays and holidays. It seemed they just couldn't handle their guilt.

Then, sometime around 1955, we entered into what would become known as the Information Age. Now with computers, Internet, cyberspace, and World Wide Web, many of us are able to work from our own homes. So it seems we've come full circle. We used to do our work at home, then we left our homes to go to work each day. Now we're coming back to our homes, and it may be we're returning to our homes to work just in the nick of time. For many of us, it truly is the eleventh hour. Uncle Sam's broke and Aunt Katie is now a successful CEO living with a significant other! So neither one of them is going to take on this responsibility. So my guess is, if you're hearing or reading this — it's your turn.

CHAPTER 2

DENIAL

K: Let's talk about denial. You say that you stayed in denial for over a year and a half. There must be lots of people who, if they weren't in denial, would recognize right now that it is their turn to take charge of things that need to be done for their parents. Could you talk to us about what denial is, and would you share some of your personal experiences?

S: I'd be happy to. Once, when I just happened to visit my folks, I pulled into their drive and noticed smoke coming from their kitchen. My parents were nowhere to be seen. I went into their house just in time to turn the stove off before it caught fire. It wasn't that my mother had forgotten she had left a pot cooking on the stove, my mother didn't even remember she had put a pot on the stove. The pot had actually melted into the burner. But you know, this had to happen several more times, and they had to fall on more than one occasion, before I was willing to admit they needed to live closer to me so I could check on them frequently. I was unwilling to admit they could no longer live alone. So I got my folks to agree to move to a neighborhood near me — one that had lots of close neighbors. In September, 1993, I moved my mother and stepfather to the same town where I lived. I thought, by moving them closer to me, I could provide the additional assistance they needed and they could continue living fairly independently. Had I not been in denial, I would have recognized immediately that they were in need of greater care and of supervision, not just assistance.

K: So, there were obvious red flags all the way along.

S: There were lots of red flags that screamed, "These people are no longer able to take care of themselves." However, I just disregarded all indicators.

K: I loved the story about the pets. Could you share that with us?

S: The story about the pets does start out to be fairly funny. Since I recognized the value of elderly people having pets, I wanted my parents to have their pets with them. We have a leash law in our town which prohibits pets from running up and down the streets. So I paid to have the yard of their new house fenced to accommodate their pets.

K: Now you say, pets; were there a lot of pets?

S: There were a LOT of pets! When I tell you we moved some of their pets, *some* is the operative word. My folks had lived in a rural environment for a number of years and they had many animals they lovingly referred to as their "pets." They had dogs, cats, ducks, chickens, turkeys, goats, pigs, and an occasional raccoon, opossum or snake. I knew we couldn't move all those animals into a city neighborhood, so I talked with my folks and we agreed to move two dogs and five cats with them. We found good homes for the rest of their animals.

K: Even the snakes and the opossum?

S: Unfortunately, a snake had taken up residence in one of the flower pots and got moved into their new living room by mistake. I am terribly afraid of snakes, so just getting that snake out of their living room was a traumatic experience for me. Another thing I was unprepared for was the fact that one of their dogs was pregnant. In a short period of time, we went from having two dogs and five cats to eleven dogs and five cats. For several weeks, I was called at my office on a daily basis to handle some crisis about these pets. I was called by my mother who informed me some of the puppies had crawled underneath the fence. They were stuck in drains and ditches and she wanted me to come free them. I was called by neighbors who reported some of the puppies were in their carports, crying, others were under cars and wouldn't come out, and other puppies were running up and down the streets. Cars had to drive on the edges of yards to keep from hitting them.

> I thought, by moving them closer to me, I could provide the additional assistance they needed...

K: How many puppies are we talking about here?

S: Nine.

K: You are a saint.

S: Two adult dogs, five cats and nine little puppies. Well, I was also called by city officials who informed me the leash law had to be complied with. I was called by other neighbors who complained the cats were climbing on their cars and leaving scratches. Then one day, a neighbor, who sounded hysterical, called and told me when she tried to put two of the puppies back over the fence, into my mother's yard, my mother thought she was taking the puppies away. So my mother came toward the lady with a pair of scissors. Of course, I left immediately and went to my mother's house. Mother confirmed the story that she had tried to attack the neighbor with a pair of scissors then threatened the woman again. I was extremely embarrassed. The woman my mother had tried to attack was the wife of one of the professors at our state university. He was a man I liked and respected, plus, he and his wife had been very kind and helpful to my folks. But you know, Kathryn, besides being embarrassed, I was scared by my mother's behavior. I knew if my mother continued to have those types of outbursts, she could be committed to a psychiatric hospital. At the very least, she might be admitted to an Alzheimer's unit. Realizing that, I worked very hard to get all those pets taken care of. We put an ad in the paper and soon found homes for all the puppies. We were back to two dogs and five cats. I truly enjoyed the peace of not having to deal with those pets. However, I was still in denial. I was unwilling to consider the notion that my parents could not function on their own. They certainly could not take care of pets.

> I look back and realize how being in denial could have cost my parents their lives.

K: I can't imagine you could even have dealt with that. Here you are a professional woman, but you tell it now with great humor, as though it were a funny story.

S: Carol Burnett once said that comedy is tragedy, plus time. There has been enough time now, since some of my tragedies, to turn them into comedy. Some of the funniest stories I now remember are the ones which seemed horrific at the time they were happening. But I'll tell you what's not funny, and that's when I look back and realize how being in denial could have cost my parents their lives.

K: We all talk about denial and I think most people have some understanding about it, but what is it really? Is it common for people to be in denial about their parents' ability to simply take care of themselves? Put on your psychologist hat for a moment.

S: Yes, it is common for caregivers to be in denial of their parents' true level of functioning. Actually, Kathryn, denial is just a way of coping. Sometimes, when things are emotionally painful, we hide behind a wall of denial in order to take care of ourselves.

K: What's so bad about being in denial?

S: I'm not saying denial is bad. Denial may be beneficial in protecting us from emotional pain. However, it may also be debilitating. It may keep us from taking any action at all. At the very least, denial influences our judgment, which may cause a multitude of other problems. It did for me and my folks.

K: **I'm still not sure I understand. Can we go one step further?**

S: Yes. Let's talk about families in terms of a systems approach. Families are actually systems made up of organized patterns of beliefs, attitudes and behaviors. Those basic beliefs serve as a structure for relationships within a family and those beliefs are formed around rules — rules either spoken or unspoken — rules everyone within the family agrees to operate within. However, sometimes the foundation of those beliefs changes, yet family members continue with those same beliefs, attitudes, and behaviors they held prior to the fundamental change. Although one, or maybe all, of the family members realize something is different, they pretend nothing has changed. This unwillingness to adapt to the change is referred to as denial. Denial usually has several layers that serve to protect those basic beliefs that are no longer true.

> I didn't want them dependent on me. I didn't want to be the caregiver.

K: **Now I'm going to ask you to take off your psychologist hat and give us an example.**

S: Kathryn, if we use an artichoke as a metaphor, we might envision the heart of the artichoke as the false belief held to be true by family members. It might have been that the belief was true at one time. It's no longer true, yet, the belief is still present. Just as with the heart of the artichoke, there are several layers of protection — leaves that have to be peeled away in order to get down to the belief. As with the artichoke, in order to get to the belief that is driving the denial, layer after layer has to be peeled away.

K: **What was your situation in your family?**

S: My mother and stepfather had an image of themselves as being strong, healthy, and independent. This could be likened to the heart of the artichoke. That was their basic belief. That image was true for them until they were about 75 years old. I also maintained that false belief about them. Consequently, our attitudes and behaviors continued to support that belief, which was no longer true. They couldn't take care of themselves. My mother, stepfather and I all conspired in this unspoken agreement to continue operating within a belief system that was not based in current reality. We all behaved as though the original belief was still true. We failed to acknowledge that something within our family had changed. My mother and stepfather were no longer strong, they were no longer in good health, they were no longer capable of being independent. This change had occurred at the very heart of our family system. Yet even in the face of much evidence to the contrary, we continued to interact in the same ways we had for years. We pretended things were just as they had always been. None of us wanted to be first to admit some change had occurred. If we admitted our belief was no longer true, then our attitudes and the way we interacted with each other would have had to change. We were operating in this superficial comfort zone none of us wanted to leave.

K: I understand what you're saying clinically, as a psychologist, but what I'm also hearing is that if you had admitted what bad shape your parents were in, they would have lost their independence and you would have lost yours. Isn't that true?

S: I'm sure that was true at some level. However, none of us were conscious of that. Looking back on it, sure, that was true. I didn't want them dependent on me. I didn't want to be the caregiver. When we don't want things to change, it seems easy to look the other way and ignore all the red flags that scream something is wrong with the picture.

K: Besides protecting us from emotional pain, are there other reasons denial seems to occur within families?

S: Yes. One reason denial exists is to maintain the status quo within the family system. When things are at the status quo, nothing has to change. As long as family members agree to deny anything has changed, they can continue to behave and interact as though things are just as they've always been. Therefore, the family system remains intact, although it may not be working very well. In many ways, denial seems to be a passive way out. People, in general, do not like change and are likely to take the path of least resistance. As long as individuals pretend things haven't changed, they don't have to exert the effort required to modify a set pattern of behaving and interacting. Denial may also exist because people fear the unknown. Even though things are not as good as individuals would want them to be, at least everyone in the family knows the spoken or unspoken rules. Therefore, with some degree of accuracy, they may predict what could happen. Often that seems preferable to the unknown.

> As long as we look the other way and stick our heads in the sand, we don't have to do anything.

K: Can you give us an example of how denial protects us from emotional pain?

S: Sure. The losses associated with growing old are many and may be extremely painful. Denying certain signs of aging may enable individuals to buffer themselves from the realization that things are not as they were in the past. Denial may protect them from the pain of looking at their lives and realizing things will probably never be as they were.

K: You say denial influences our judgment. What do you mean by that?

S: The most obvious problem with denial is that denial is a distortion of information. Remember, denial occurs when some belief that used to be true is no longer true, yet individuals continue to believe it's true. That's distortion. In order to make informed decisions, we need accurate information, not distorted information. Decisions based on inaccurate information are usually not good decisions. Sometimes people make decisions based on something that was true a long time ago. They don't look closely at the present situation and see that it's no longer true. Sometimes denial keeps people from taking any action at all. As long as we look the other way and stick our heads in the sand, we don't have to do anything. For example, I wouldn't have to worry about taking away Carl's truck keys because the hazard wouldn't exist if I refused to look. Carried to its extreme, denial creates situations that are dangerous and sometimes even cost people their lives.

K: So you said to yourself, "It can't be true," rather than saying, "It is true." Could you share with us your personal situation again, if we could go back to that? Maybe some of your own personal story when you were in denial.

S: My mother and stepfather were about 75 years old. And as I mentioned, they lived in a rural area. Their nearest neighbors were about a quarter of a mile from their house. I had known for several years that they were gradually declining. They were becoming less and less able to take care of themselves. But I wanted them to stay strong. I wanted them to stay healthy. I wanted them to remain independent. The last thing I wanted was to have to take care of two other adults. I denied all the signals. Yet it became increasingly obvious these people could not take care of themselves. As I mentioned, they fell on several occasions and we attributed those falls to any number of reasons. Our unspoken rule was that none of us would admit they could no longer walk or see or hear as well as they used to. At an unspoken level, we agreed not to talk about it, not address those issues.

> The rug was loose. The light wasn't on. It was never their fault.

K: So did you just ignore it? Did you flat ignore it?

S: Not only did we ignore the truth, we came up with reasons to justify why the accidents were not their fault. The rug was loose. The light wasn't on. It was never their fault. We created a whole fabric of reasons to explain why they fell and how Mother could have kept forgetting the stove was on. Do you see how denial works?

K: Yes, I understand now.

S: If any of us had admitted they could no longer see or hear or walk as well as they used to, then our roles — our family relationships — would have to change. My relationship with them as a daughter would then change; I would become the caregiver. Their status of independence would change to one of dependence, if we came out of denial.

K: I also hear, if anyone admitted it, they may have to take charge.

S: Ironically, one of the things that happens, as individuals get closer to the time they will need to take charge of their parents, is that they stop visiting them as often. They don't want to see it. The red flags keep getting bigger and redder, and screaming something needs to be done. So, if they visit their parents, they run the risk of seeing those flags. It really is ironic that the closer we move toward it, the further away we want to get. In our case, we just did nothing. The next disaster, for us, occurred on a Sunday. My stepfather still had, but should not have had, his driver's license. He drove Mother to their old neighborhood to see one of the neighbors she had given her chickens to. The lady gave three of the chickens back to Mother. Well, Mother brought the chickens to her new house. She then killed and cleaned those chickens on her front porch. Now, it might help if I remind you that my mother is a very Southern lady who grew up on a farm during the Depression. She thought nothing of wringing a chicken's neck, putting it in a pot of boiling water, and plucking the feathers off of it. She intended to cook those chickens.

> I realized my mother could no longer safely prepare meals. It wasn't even safe for her to be around a stove.

K: This was in the condominium in Tallahassee?

S: This was in a town house with lots of neighbors. Not only were chickens not allowed, due to city ordinance, but several of the neighborhood children had gathered to see what this old woman was doing to those chickens. They had never seen a chicken killed before, much less on someone's front porch. The first news I got of it was when one of the children's mothers called and asked me if my mother was performing some sort of Satanic ritual. I asked her not to call the police and assured her I would take care of it immediately.

K: You seem to have maintained a wonderful sense of humor about all of this.

S: Kathryn, you have to; you just have to keep a sense of humor. From the safe distance afforded me by time, I can now enjoy these stories. However, I also realize the serious implications my denial could have had. While I was solving problems associated with pets and chickens, there were other problems occurring that were much more serious. I realized my mother could no longer safely prepare meals. It wasn't even safe for her to be around a stove. So I enlisted a community service to transport my folks to a senior citizens' center. They would go there every day to eat lunch and engage in other social activities. However, within a month's time, their health had declined such that traveling to the center was no longer an option. At that point, I enlisted the services of a wonderful organization that brings meals to elderly people who are housebound.

K: Do most cities have that?

S: Yes they do. You might call a local elder care office. They're usually listed in the white pages of phone directories, and are happy to refer you to those services. I have also included phone numbers here in the Resources section. Well, this wonderful service brought more food to my parents than any four people could eat. And as I've said, my mother was a Southern lady who came through the Depression. She understood the importance of not wasting food. Of course, she wouldn't waste anything else for that matter. Her motto was, "Waste not, want not." Not only did she save every styrofoam container the food came in, but she also saved every salt and pepper packet and every bit of food. She refused to eat the fresh food until all the old food was gone. Now, I'm all for conservation, and this may not seem such a big problem. It may even solicit commendation from some, but there was another problem. We live in Florida and my mother would mistakenly turn on the heat for the air conditioning. It was not uncommon for the temperature in their house to be over 100° Fahrenheit. Well, you can imagine what happened. I had to go over there twice a day to try to prevent them from getting food poisoning. I tried to keep all the old food discarded. And here was another thing; my mother would become upset if she saw me throwing anything out. I would often have to call my sister to come help. Then one of us would entertain our folks while the other went to the kitchen and threw all this stuff away. Well, we were very creative and thought we had solved the problem.

> Not only did she save every styrofoam container the food came in, but she also saved every salt and pepper packet and every bit of food.

K: Why did you think you had creatively solved the problem?

S: Because we were going over there and dumping all of this stuff, not just in the garbage can in her kitchen, but we were taking all this stuff out to the street to a big dumpster. We were getting rid of all the old food, so they would only have fresh food, right? Let me tell you what happened. Within a few days, Mother caught on to what we were doing. She started going outside to the dumpster, getting the old food out, bringing it back inside, and carrying on with her plan to consume the old food first.

K: Let me guess — you and your sister were both in denial about your mother?

S: That's probably the understatement of the year.

K: So then what did you do? What's the rest of the story here?

S: Well, my sister and I continued in our fight against the food and styrofoam boxes. We won some of the battles, but we were losing the war. There was no way we could keep up with all this, so I hired a cleaning service to come twice a week to help keep the old food discarded. That didn't work very well, either. Do you know what I finally had to do? I had to go to my mother's house every day and take her garbage home with me to keep her from going outside and getting the old food and bringing it back in. And guess what? I was still not willing to reconsider my belief that they could live alone.

K: Dr. Haymon, you've been remarkably honest about your own personal denial regarding your parents' situation with cooking pots, pets, old food, and whatever. Was driving a big issue with your stepfather, Carl?

S: Kathryn, it was a huge issue. For most of his life, he drove a taxi for a living. He enjoyed driving. After he retired from that job, he went to work for the government. He drove a truck for the forestry department. Driving was who he was; that's how he identified himself and he was very proud of that. He had a wonderful driving record, but the truth is, not only could he not see or hear well, his circulation was very poor. Sometimes he had leg cramps so severe he could hardly use the brakes on his truck. Several times I asked him not to drive. I stopped by at least once a day to take him and my mother to the grocery store or wherever they wanted to go. Yet he still continued to drive when I wasn't there, not only on neighborhood streets, but he continued to drive on the interstate. Then, one night, I came home from a business meeting to retrieve several phone messages. One of the messages was from a deputy sheriff who said my folks had been in an accident but were not injured. He had checked their address and saw that they were only about five blocks from their house. Now remember, we live in Florida. About 26% of our population is over 65. This deputy sheriff was quite used to seeing elderly people driving.

> The street they lived on was only two blocks long, yet neither my mother nor stepfather could remember which house was theirs.

So when he saw they were only a few blocks from their house, he released them to drive themselves home. The next message I got was from a state trooper who said my parents were driving on the wrong side of the road when he stopped them. They were northbound in the southbound lane of a two-lane street. He had called the number on my business card. The telephone rang into an answering service for the mental health agency where I worked. Since I couldn't be reached, my boss was contacted, and the third message was from him. He said he and his wife had picked up my parents and driven them home. Although my boss knew what street my folks lived on, he didn't know their house number. It was very sad, Kathryn, it was very sad. He told me he drove up and down the street for about thirty minutes because my folks couldn't remember which house they lived in. The street they lived on was only two blocks long, yet neither my mother nor stepfather could remember which house was theirs. I realized they were upset about the accident and the state trooper. They were anxious and nervous.

K: Umhum, sounds like you were in denial again.

S: I was still explaining how it was not their fault. Denial is exactly what was going on.

K: I hear you saying it right now.

S: I guess I still explain it that way. Anyway, they had this little aluminum boat and finally my mother said, "Oh, that's our boat, that's our boat. That's where we live." My boss made sure they got into their house safely. His message also stated he had left their truck at a service station. I got a friend to go with me that night and take the truck to their house. I talked with my folks and comforted them. My stepfather had been cited for a violation. What had happened was that they had gone to a grocery store near their house. This store was located in a strip mall with many other shops and stores and lots of pedestrian traffic. While he was backing out of his parking space, he mistook the accelerator for the brake. Another car was traveling behind him. Poor Carl; he thought his foot was on the brake and he just floored it. Kathryn, he knocked the moving car into a parked car and that car into a tree. When I read the accident report the following day, I cried. I realized if somebody, if some child, had been walking behind Carl's truck, she or he would have been killed. I had no choice; I took his truck keys and cried again. I did not want to take away this grown man's independence, but I had no choice. I could no longer deny he wasn't safe to drive.

> It's really tough to make decisions that take away another adult's independence.

K: Was that one of the first tough decisions you had to make?

S: It's really tough to make decisions that take away another adult's independence. The decisions I had to make in the next layer of denial presented even further health risks for my parents. Even after all this, we continued to maintain our family relationships just the way they had always been. Since my stepfather was mentally more alert than my mother, he assumed responsibility for their medications. Unfortunately, he kept confusing their medicines. He'd take hers and he'd give her his, or they'd both take too much one day and wouldn't take any the next day. I thought, if I could just explain it more clearly to him, he would be able to handle this. Stuck in denial, I relied on my own creativity.

K: You were going to save the day again, I can see it coming.

S: Absolutely. I could fix this one. I knew I could fix this one. So guess what I did? Once a week, I would sit down with them and explain their medications. I would put appropriate doses in separate envelopes — one for each day of the week for each of them. Now that's real simple isn't it? Well, compliance with using the envelopes lasted only a few days. I went over there one afternoon and realized they had taken the medication intended for an entire week in just two days. I was bewildered. I didn't know what to do. I was frustrated. I had solved a lot of problems in my life, but I didn't know what to do with this. Then, one day, I was at the pharmacy. I was standing there, waiting for their prescriptions to be filled, when I saw what I thought must have been the most ingenious invention in the whole world. There it was! A plastic box with

They had taken the medication intended for an entire week in just two days.

seven columns and four compartments in each column. This would work! There was a column for each day of the week and a compartment for morning, one for noon, one for afternoon, and one for evening. All they'd have to do was slide this little drawer out and take the medicine from each compartment. I bought two of them. I went racing over to my mother's house. I was so excited! I'm not kidding you. I was thrilled!

K: Solve the problems and they can stay at home. I can see it coming.

S: I was so excited to show them these boxes. I explained how it worked. I went over this in detail. I wrote Mother's name on the front of one box. I put Carl's name on the other. Guess what? About three days later, I realized this wasn't working any better than the envelopes had. I knew they could not continue taking prescribed medication in this haphazard manner. It was dangerous for them. They weren't supposed to be taking each other's medication. They weren't supposed to be taking a whole week's worth in two days and taking none at all for three or four days, yet I knew I couldn't go over there four times a day.

K: Did it ever come to mind that maybe you should put them in a nursing home when you were consumed by caregiving, or were you in such denial you just couldn't face it?

S: No. That thought never occurred to me. I just thought it was me. I kept thinking, somehow, I could get this right. I could take care of everything, which would allow them to live independently. I tried really hard, but it seemed it couldn't be done.

K: You were so good at maintaining their situation through your denial. What finally jump-started you into doing something about it?

S: What finally shocked me out of denial happened that infamous Valentine's Day, 1994. That was five months, which seemed like five years, after I had moved my folks near me. And, Kathryn, I'm not exaggerating; if you multiplied all the things I've talked about by ten, you still would have only the tip of the iceberg of problems I dealt with. Here's what finally happened: At that time, I was completing a residency in psychology. I normally stopped by to see my folks on my way to work, or went over there during my lunch hour. However, I had gone to work early that morning, so I did not stop by my mother's house. On that particular day, I had seen clients back to back and had not even taken a lunch break. I had not seen or talked to my folks since the previous afternoon, so I called my mother to find out how they were doing. I also wanted to let her know I would come by there right after work, but that I would probably be working until about eight o'clock that night. I had Valentine candy and I had little presents for them. It was important for me to go by and take those to them. When I asked my mother how they were, she said she was fine but Carl had gone to bed late the previous afternoon and had not gotten up since. Well, I quickly calculated that Carl had been in bed nearly 24 hours. I asked her if he had talked to her, and she said, "Well, I talked to him several times, but he didn't answer. He didn't say anything." I said, "Mother, is he breathing?" She said, " I don't know." I was just shocked! I said, "Mother, please go see if you can get him to respond and stay right there with him." Well, my sister is a registered nurse and she worked at a hospital near their house. So I called her and explained the situation because I knew she could get there quicker than I could. I asked her to please go over there and see what was going on. She did, and within a matter of minutes, she called back and told me Carl was breathing but he was not verbally responding. She said she had already called for paramedics and, as soon as they came and took Carl to the hospital, she would take Mother home with her. I told her I would meet the paramedics at the hospital. It was during those next few hours that I was asked all those questions about CPR, hospitalization, and advance directives. I was overwhelmed. I so wished that I had not stayed in denial. I wished I had somehow admitted that day was coming — that it was already there. Being in an emergency room was hardly the time or place for me to be trying to figure all this out. Anyway, sometime around midnight, all the questions had been answered, I had filled out all the forms, and Carl was resting in the hospital. I remember walking out to my car and another shock hit me. I thought, oh my goodness, what am I going to do with Mother?

> Being in an emergency room was hardly the time or place for me to be trying to figure all this out.

K: Oh, boy. Where was Mother?

S: My sister, Wanda, had taken Mother home with her. So I called my sister and she said it was okay for Mother to spend the night with her, but I would need to come and get her first thing the following morning because she would have to go to work. Well, you see, I lived alone and worked 15-hour days because I was trying to finish a residency. Even if I moved my mother home with me, there would be nobody there the majority of time to even see about her. Knowing her history of turning on stoves and the unfamiliarity of my house, I knew she couldn't be left alone. I felt guilty because I thought she needed to come home with me, but that was not an option. I felt so overwhelmed. The next morning, I started calling care facilities. Not only did I find out they didn't have any rooms or even any bed space, but I learned that they had waiting lists that were months long!

K: When you say care facilities, would most people know that to be nursing homes?

S: Actually, I didn't call any nursing homes because I couldn't admit my mother needed nursing home care, even though she did. She and Carl both needed to have been in full nursing home care months prior to that event. Instead, I called several adult congregate living facilities. Those accommodations are like small apartments. Individuals have their own large bedrooms and bathrooms, but they don't have kitchens because they aren't allowed to have stoves. There is usually a large dining room where residents eat prepared meals together. I called these types of facilities because I was still in denial about my mother's true level of functioning. I was only willing to admit Mother couldn't live alone and I had to find a place for her to live.

K: And did you find one finally?

S: Yes. I found a facility that had a room and I told them immediately that we'd take it. Then came the next eye-opener for me. The lady said, "We'll have to interview and evaluate your mother. Then we will decide whether you take this room or not." That was a real shock for me. I had so many choices about other things, yet I didn't really have a choice about that, nor did I have any idea what "to evaluate" meant. I only knew I wanted my mom to pass whatever evaluation so that she would have a place to live. My mother and I arrived early for our screening at this care facility. When the admissions director met with me, I felt like I had been dropped off on another planet and I didn't speak the language. She was a tall young woman in her late twenties, with blond hair and blue eyes. She wore glasses and was either plump or pregnant, I couldn't tell which because of the oversized top she was wearing. She was pleasant and, after a short introduction, she opened a folder. Without even looking up or taking a breath, here's what she said: "You do understand this is an ACLF. I see that your mother has SS. Does she have A and B? Does she have SSI? How about OSS?"

> I started calling care facilities…but I learned that they had waiting lists that were months long!

K: Whoa.

S: I was stunned. I was stunned. I had never heard so many acronyms in my whole life. I had no idea what she was even talking about. I guess she could feel me staring at her, because she looked up over her glasses, just for a second, and then she continued. She said, "Is she eligible for the Medicaid Medically Needy Program?" Kathryn, I was paralyzed. I was caught somewhere between not having a clue as to what she was talking about and wanting desperately to respond appropriately so she would accept my mother. I'm not sure how long I sat there, staring into space. I was hoping that somewhere in all of my life's experiences I had recorded some information in long term memory that would at least help me fake this one. Then the next thing I heard was, "You will need proof of your mother's eligibility for these programs, otherwise private pay is $1,935 a month."

K: Oh my. How much?

S: Nineteen hundred and thirty-five dollars a month. Kathryn, I was completing a residency. I didn't even make that much money a month.

K: That's not including the medical costs and expenses Carl needed at the hospital?

S: Oh no, this was just for my mother. I was so overwhelmed. I could feel my eyes tearing, yet I knew I didn't have the luxury of crying. Even if I did, who was going to comfort me? My mother sat there with this childlike smile on her face. She didn't know what day it was or what was happening. She really didn't even know what was going on. I remember she looked at me so trustingly. I could no longer deny our roles had reversed. It was now, indeed, my turn to parent her. So I took a deep breath and swallowed the lump in my throat. Then I admitted to this admissions director, "This is my first experience in taking care of my parents and I don't know what to do. I want to do a good job. I just don't know where to start." I continued, " Quite frankly, I don't even know what you're talking about." She was kind enough to write down all those acronyms, all those fragments of the alphabet I didn't understand. She agreed to evaluate my mother since we were already there. She passed! We were then told they would hold the room for her until the next day. At that time, we either had to produce approved eligibility forms, or we had to agree to private pay if she was to have the room. Then this very kind woman directed me to the appropriate state agencies. This was the day after Carl was admitted to the hospital and I had been up until after midnight in the emergency room with him. I was tired and I needed to be at work. Anyway, during the next few hours, I felt as though I were in a time warp with all these aliens speaking this strange language. I met with representatives from a number of state agencies and I explained our situation. I explained it over and over and over to different people in different departments. Kathryn, I filled out forms until my eyes were crossed, plus I had to make several trips to get birth certificates, bank statements, and copies of Medicare cards. I even had to produce an itemized statement of all their personal belongings.

> ...she looked at me so trustingly. I could no longer deny our roles had reversed.

K: This was all the day after Carl went into the hospital? That's unbelievable. I'll bet you were glad you'd gone through the purses when you moved them.

S: I don't know what I would have done if I had not at least done that. By late that afternoon, I was told everything looked to be in order but they needed to interview my mother prior to approving her for assistance.

K: So you did find assistance? You had a place for her to go and you were able to get assistance?

S: Yes, if she passed this last interview.

K: Another test to go through? Goodness sakes.

S: I looked at the clock, I had about thirty minutes to drive across town, get my mother, and drive back to this state office before they closed. I was so frustrated. Not one of these people I had been providing information to — and there were many — not one of them ever indicated they would need to talk to my mother. If I had known that, I could have brought Mother back with me during one of the trips when I was running back and forth getting all those documents. No, they waited until thirty minutes before closing to tell me they had to interview her. Remember, the care facility was only going to hold the bed for her until the following morning. So I didn't have the luxury of waiting to do this the next day. Once again, I had to stuff my feelings. I couldn't afford to vent my frustrations. These people had power. They held the magic

> I couldn't take in any new information that contradicted my basic belief that my folks were strong, healthy, in control, and could live alone.

pen that could just as easily check the "rejected" box as the "approved" box. I thanked them profusely and promised I would be back with my mother before they closed. Then, Kathryn, I literally ran — physically ran — out of the state building. I got into my car, I drove as fast as I could, I picked up my mother, and drove back across town. I got into the state building and had five minutes to spare. They interviewed her, and guess what? She passed! We had the assistance and we had a room. I was thrilled with all of this! With the approved forms in my hand, I called the care facility and announced my mother and I were en route to the furniture store to purchase the furniture they had specified and would be there within a couple of hours. This particular facility required specific furniture — single beds, night stands, and chests-of-drawers, but not dressers. I had to pay the furniture delivery men extra money on the side to get them to deliver the furniture, since it was after hours.

K: Luckily you had the $2,000 from the purses to buy the furniture. Good thinking.

S: And the filing cabinet! Well, as I moved my mother in, I had to face another painful belief I had not really looked at. I believed that nursing homes represented the last place prior to death. I guess that belief originated in my childhood when we placed my grandmother in a nursing home and she died a couple of years later. I supposed that I could postpone my parents' deaths by postponing a nursing home. Even though this first placement was not a nursing home, it was an assisted living facility, I still had to face the fact that my parents would never live alone again. Now you're probably wondering, at this time, how I could have continued to ignore such blatantly obvious signs, signs which clearly indicated my mother and stepfather were incapable of living on their own. The answer is quite simple: I was in denial. And while in denial, I couldn't take in any new information that contradicted my basic belief that my folks were strong, healthy, in control, and could live alone. You see, that's what denial does. It blocks us from any information that contradicts our basic belief, whether the belief is true or not.

Kathryn, there is another level of my denial I feel I need to talk about, because it's so prevalent in many families, and that is the level of denial that is created by alcoholism. As a matter of fact, the percentage of elderly patients seeking medical treatment that are actually alcoholic, may be as high as 20%. And maybe 40% of the elderly people admitted to veteran's hospitals have a lifetime diagnosis of alcoholism.

K: I had no idea it was that significant.

S: My guess is the percentages are actually higher, for a couple of reasons. First of all, families are in denial about alcoholism, and especially when it's Grandma or Grandpa, so they don't talk to their physicians about it. Unfortunately, alcoholism among the elderly often goes undiagnosed because elderly people are often not screened for alcoholism. Sometimes they are diagnosed with depression, dementia, or Alzheimer's, when in fact many of their symptoms are created by alcohol. So the symptoms are treated, rather than the problem.

> ...elderly people are often not screened for alcoholism. Sometimes they are diagnosed with depression, dementia, or Alzheimer's, when in fact many of their symptoms are created by alcohol.

K: Were both of your parents alcoholic?

S: Yes, both my mother and stepfather were severely alcoholic, and my biological father had also been alcoholic before he died. Consequently, having grown up with alcoholic parents, I had learned from a very early age to deny reality. It's like the example in the book, An Elephant in the Living Room, by Marion H. Typpo. The elephant is actually the drinking — the alcoholism, yet everybody pretends the elephant isn't there. There is a child in the story who sees the elephant and wonders why nobody else does. The child tries to talk about it, but no one in the family is willing to validate this child's reality. So the child learns to pretend there's no elephant. Nobody else sees it. Nobody's willing to talk about it. So she denies the elephant is there. The unspoken rule was to not admit there was an elephant in the living room and to not talk about it. So the child learns to not trust herself. She sees it, but nobody else validates that for her, so she learns to walk around it.

K: Dr. Haymon, I can see how this would have been even more difficult for you, and that you would be more likely to be in denial, given the fact that you were an adult child of alcoholic parents.

S: My mother continued drinking until she was in her mid-seventies and my stepfather continued drinking until the time he was actually moved to a nursing home. Remember I told you my folks fell several times and some of those falls resulted in broken bones? Not one time did I ever attribute any of their falls to their alcoholism. I pretended, of course, that it was the loose rug or the light not being on. And probably much of their confusion and forgetfulness was actually due to alcohol. Yet my folks and I continued in our denial. Not one time did we ever talk about the elephant in our living room.

K: You really spent a lifetime participating in denial with your parents, didn't you?

S: Kathryn, it was difficult for me to distinguish between situational behaviors related to alcohol and behaviors associated with irreversible dementia. Although I'm a psychologist, it was still difficult for me to sort that out. Growing up with alcoholic parents, I learned to live a lifetime of denying. Anything you don't really want to see, you just pretend isn't there. You do that by sticking your head in the sand, or by putting on rose colored glasses. You look the other way. You call black white and white black. You do whatever it takes to avoid situations you've been taught to ignore and maybe even been punished for seeing.

> Not one time did I ever attribute any of their falls to their alcoholism. I pretended, of course, that it was the loose rug or the light not being on.

K: I can see how denial keeps people from placing their parents in a care facility, but why would you ask your 70- or 80-year-old parent to stop drinking so late in life?

S: That's a good question. I think my story paints a very clear picture why. You might have no other choice than to place them in a care facility, and, Kathryn, that's when they may have to stop drinking, or smoking, or using tobacco, because some facilities don't allow the use of alcohol or tobacco. My parents were in an adult living facility and the residents who lived there were expected to be somewhat independent and responsible. For the most part, this facility didn't mind if residents had a beer or a glass of wine, but Carl was alcoholic. He couldn't stop with a beer. He couldn't stop with two beers. Carl's a Southern man who grew up on a farm. He's "country" and wears overalls, bib overalls. He would go next door and buy a six pack and stick cans of beer in every pocket he had. He would come waddling back to the facility thinking nobody noticed, even though he looked like he had gained forty pounds since he left.

K: Umhum, he's clever.

S: Alcoholics are. That's a really good way to put it. When individuals are addicted to any substance, they become very clever, very creative, in figuring out ways to get that need met. Well, his beer drinking really wasn't causing any problems. I think the people at the facility just sort of looked the other way. Here's this old man who just wants to have his beer. He's not rowdy. He's not hurting anybody, so they just let him get away with it. And he did get away with it for several months. Then, one day, he paid somebody to bring him a bottle of whiskey. And Kathryn, not only did he get drunk, but he got my mother drunk. He was out pushing my mother in her wheelchair, which he liked to do, and it was good exercise for him. He would push her up and down the driveway in front of the facility. Then, when he was going up the driveway toward the street, he just decided to leave with her. My mother had this bottle of whiskey between her legs in the wheelchair. Carl had taken several drinks and he had given my mother several drinks. My mother was sort of out of it, and she didn't really understand a lot. The first news the head nurse at this facility got that my parents had even left the premises was when the police called and said there was this old man pushing an old woman in a wheelchair a few blocks from the facility. Mother and Carl were at the intersection of a four-lane highway. Naturally, the police figured that they had wandered off from this facility. Kathryn, that was one of the most frightening experiences for me. Carl pushed my mother along this four lane highway, which is at a 30-degree incline. All he would have had to do was slip or stumble and my mother would have gone flying out into the middle of four lanes of traffic. Not only could she have been killed, but she could have been so severely injured that she might have had to lie in the hospital and suffer for days, weeks or months. I was not surprised when I was asked to move my folks. Care facilities just cannot accept that kind of liability.

> When individuals are addicted to any substance, they become very clever, very creative in figuring out ways to get that need met.

K: So then what did you do?

S: I had to find another place for them to live. However, this time I knew they needed to go into a nursing home. I was finally able to admit they were not appropriate for congregate, community living. I knew, even if I could get them into another facility, it would only be a matter of time before I would be dealing with similar problems, if they lived that long. I knew they needed to be in a facility that had 24-hour nursing care. Once again, I was very fortunate because I was able to find a nursing home where I could move both of them at the same time. The good news was, I thought, the nursing home did not allow alcohol. The sad news was, even though Carl's physician knew he was alcohol-dependent, he did not prescribe treatment for alcohol withdrawal. So, within a couple of weeks, Carl had become so agitated, so combative, he had to be admitted to a psychiatric unit. Well, he stayed there for a couple of weeks and received treatment. He was then dismissed and returned to the nursing home. Less than two weeks later, he was back in the psychiatric hospital. He stayed there for two more weeks. During that time, guess what? I was notified that I had to move him to an Alzheimer's facility. His acting-out behavior was attributed to irreversible dementia. The closest we ever came to addressing his alcoholism was when the attending physician said it was okay for Carl to have non-alcoholic beer. Kathryn, placebos work in a lot of situations. However, alcoholism is not the place to be using a placebo. I couldn't find local placement for him, so I had to move him to another part of the state. Not only did this mean he and my mother had to be separated, but putting him in an Alzheimer's unit created yet another problem. He was not allowed to continue using tobacco there.

> I would never want another elderly person to be asked to give up a lifetime habit of drinking or smoking without being properly treated for withdrawal.

K: So he really wasn't treated for tobacco withdrawal either?

S: No, and I want to cry every time I think about what this man went through. Kathryn, he was asked to withdraw from a 70-year habit of using tobacco, without nicotine patches or any treatment at all for withdrawal from nicotine. It was horrible. The poor man was not only suffering from alcohol withdrawal, he now had to withdraw from nicotine. You know, it truly is a miracle he lived through it. Some individuals don't. Many people question issues of alcohol and tobacco with elderly people. Perhaps they think, well, they're probably only going to live a couple more years, so why even bother? This is why.

In my denial, I made a lot of mistakes. There is no doubt about it. I cannot go back and correct those mistakes, but I'll tell you what, I did learn a lot. Now I've become an advocate for elderly people. Kathryn, I truly want others to benefit from my mistakes, in hopes this will not happen to them or to their loved ones. I would never want another elderly person to be asked to give up a lifetime habit of drinking or smoking without being properly treated for withdrawal. I have created a Red Flag Checklist to help other people do a reality check. In that list, I've included specific red flags for those family members who may have a history of alcohol or tobacco use.

K: Dr. Haymon, I can see how dangerous it is for people to be in denial. I also see that much of this is still very painful for you. I want you to know how much I appreciate your courage in coming and talking about these issues, which many other people will face when it becomes their turn. Thank you so much.

CHAPTER 3

MEDICAL CHOICES

K: **Dr. Haymon, you mentioned there are many end-of-life medical decisions which we will have to make. Will you tell us more about what choices we have?**

S: First of all, I want to be very clear in telling you I am not a medical doctor; I am a psychologist. So the things I share with you and the information I offer you are based on my personal experience and on my own personal understanding of these medical decisions.

It is interesting that we are the first generation to be faced with so many medical choices. Most of the heart-wrenching decisions we have to make have to do with hospitalization, CPR, and feeding tubes, and these are all extremely difficult decisions. These decisions often create spiritual, emotional and moral struggles for many of us. My intent here is not to persuade you either way. These are very personal decisions which must be made on an individual basis. The only point I want to make is that we do have choices. However, we only have choices as long as we make these decisions in advance. As I said before, at the time, I didn't even know what an advance directive was.

> ...administering CPR to a frail, elderly patient may actually be harmful to her or him.

K: **What is an advance directive?**

S: Good question. It is a legal document that allows individuals to make their own medical decisions while they are competent to make them. One of the first choices I want to talk about is CPR.

K: **I didn't even know we had a choice about CPR.**

S: Neither did I, nor did I know administering CPR to a frail, elderly patient may actually be harmful to her or him.

Cardiopulmonary Resuscitation

K: Tell us about CPR.

S: CPR is the acronym for cardiopulmonary resuscitation. This procedure was developed in the early 1960's as a means of preventing sudden, unexpected death in cases such as drowning or electrical shock. CPR was never intended to be used in cases of terminal illness or where death was expected. Research presented at a conference for CPR and emergency cardiac care in 1974 reported that resuscitation in those cases might represent violation of a person's right to die with dignity.

K: Are there some studies that prove this?

S: In 1988, the *Journal of the American Medical Association* described CPR as an emotionally and physically traumatic procedure. You see, Kathryn, the techniques used in CPR are extremely aggressive and may be harmful, especially to frail, elderly people. Sometimes their ribs are broken, or a lung might be punctured, and brain damage could occur, due to lack of oxygen resulting from time lapse. In addition to all that, if the person is transferred to an emergency room, treatment usually becomes even more aggressive. Unless the patient has documents prohibiting the use of artificial life support, she or he could receive treatment which includes electrical shock to the heart, injections of medications intended to stimulate the heart, and she or he might even be placed on mechanical respirators, even though she or he might not have wanted that.

> ...resuscitation in those cases might represent violation of a person's right to die with dignity.

K: I really had no idea.

S: Neither did I. I think most people have no idea of the complications associated with CPR. Frail, elderly patients usually never recover from the complications of cardiopulmonary resuscitation. Using CPR on those patients severely reduces the possibility of them dying a normal and peaceful death.

K: Are there research studies that support your theory here?

S: There are many studies. In one particular study, reported in the *Journal of the American Medical Association* (1988), there were 77 patients who received CPR. All of them were over 70 years of age. Not one of them lived to be discharged from the hospital. There was another study presented in the *Journal for the American Geriatrics Society* (1990). In that study, 117 nursing home residents all received CPR.

K: How many survived?

S: Two. Those who do survive almost always have a Do Not Resuscitate order placed in their medical records afterward. Neither they, nor their families, feel the trauma and complications associated with CPR are worth it. They never want to go through that again. There are additional studies that were conducted in attempts to improve the survival rate of nursing home patients who receive CPR. In those studies, the most advanced cardiac life support systems were used. There were physicians on 24-hour duty and they had the most advanced equipment and medications. In a particular study, reported in the *Journal of the American Geriatrics Society* (1992), 45 residents received CPR. Not one of them survived to be discharged. So the conclusion is, even with the most advanced cardiac life support, the survival rate for elderly citizens does not improve. I realize these statistics are depressing. They are. But I believe, in order for us to make an informed decision about any matter, as much information as possible needs to be considered. CPR is a choice. However, for frail, elderly individuals, it may not be the best choice. And it is only a choice as long as you make that decision ahead of time. Please remember, neither paramedics, nor nurses, nor physicians will make this decision for you, no matter how seriously ill the patient is. So for those people who decide they would rather not go through the trauma and the risk of CPR, they must have a Do Not Resuscitate (DNR) order placed in their medical records. Sometimes this is called a No Code, or No CPR, or DNR, or DNRO. Some states have standard forms. In other states, you have to have your physician actually write an order. The bottom line is, if you don't want to go through the trauma of CPR, you have to have something in your medical records that prohibits CPR from being administered. This document not only needs to be in your medical records, but you also need to give a copy of it to your emergency contact person.

> Those who do survive almost always have a Do Not Resuscitate order placed in their medical records afterward.

Emergency Medical Information Kit

Another thing I have learned during my turn is that paramedics are trained to look on the refrigerator door for emergency medical information. That just makes common sense to me, and it's a simple thing to do. I have actually made it quite easy. I have created the *Sandra Haymon Refrigerator Door Emergency Medical Information Kit*. Here's what it is: It is a clear plastic pocket with magnets on the back of it. You can put whatever emergency information you want in this pocket, including your advance directives. Then you just go and, like magic, stick it to your refrigerator door.

Consent To Withhold
Cardiopulmonary Resuscitation (CPR)

I, _____, being over the legal age required by state law and of sound mind do voluntarily and intentionally make known my desire and will that Cardiopulmonary Resuscitation (CPR) **not** be initiated (as provided by state law) in the event of my cardiac and/or respiratory arrest.

Cardiopulmonary Resuscitation (CPR) has been explained to me and, I direct a *No Code* order be placed in my medical records and that Cardiopulmonary Resuscitation not be initiated.

I understand that I may revoke these directions at any time as provided by state law.

I understand the importance of this decision; I am competent to make this decision; and I voluntarily and freely sign this *No Code* directive on (date) _____ in the presence of witnesses.

Patient's Signature: _____

Print Full Name: _____

Address: _____

_____

Witness   Signature: _____

Print Full Name: _____

Address: _____

_____

Witness   Signature: _____

Print Full Name: _____

Address: _____

_____

Acknowledgment: Notarize if Required by State Law

State of _____)
)ss
County of _____)

On this date _____, before me personally appeared _____ ,
to me known to be the person described in and who executed the foregoing instrument and acknowledged to me
that (she/he) _____ executed the same as (her/his) _____ free act and deed.

_____   My commission expires: _____
        Notary Public

K: Great idea. I know my mother has made specific decisions. She has probably even filled out a living will but it's in an old trunk, under three old quilts, at the bottom of her bed. They would never find it. So what a good idea.

S: In reality, it doesn't matter what documents your mother has filled out. If nobody has access to them, and they are not part of her medical records, technically, she doesn't have any documents. I would like for everybody to have their emergency medical information on their refrigerator door. It's also a good idea, if you are taking care of an elderly loved one, to get copies of emergency medical information and keep them with you. For months, I carried every document I thought I would need for my parents in the glove compartment of my car, because I never knew when I would have to meet paramedics at an emergency room. Also, if your parents are living alone, maybe you could insist they give a copy of their emergency information to their next door neighbor. The bottom line is, we want to ensure, no matter what a person's wishes are, that those wishes will be carried out.

Heroic Measures

K: As we conclude our discussion on CPR, you have told us how to avoid having CPR and heroic measures. What if you want heroic measures? Do you have to fill out advance directives?

S: No. Some people believe every life-saving technique should be used. Without advance directives, the medical community will ensure that every possible effort is made to keep the person alive.

Hospitalization

K: Dr. Haymon, can we now talk about the choices we have regarding hospitalization of elderly individuals? Why wouldn't an elderly person want to be hospitalized?

S: I suppose I was naive, but, honestly, at the time, I didn't know we had a choice as to whether or not my parents would be hospitalized. I had assumed, regardless of their condition and no matter what the prognosis for recovery, they would go to the hospital. What I learned during my turn was that a Do Not Hospitalize Order actually protects individuals from automatically being hospitalized without first carefully considering their state of health. I also learned there are certain traumas and risks with hospitalization. For example, infections we might get in a hospital are more resistant to antibiotics and can be much more difficult to treat than infections we might get at home. Also, many elderly people become confused when they go to any unfamiliar environment. When hospitalized, they are surrounded by nurses, orderlies, aides, and other strangers. This is confusing and often creates anxiety for them. Should they become agitated, the possibility they will be put in restraints or sedated increases significantly. This is especially true for demented patients who may already be experiencing thought confusion or disorientation. There is also an increased possibility of receiving more aggressive treatment, which includes diagnostic testing, when you are in a hospital. Diagnostic tests are often invasive and may be frightening and painful to elderly people. So when you know you wouldn't treat any condition these tests might reveal, it just seems kinder to not put an older person through this trauma.

> So when you know you wouldn't treat any condition these tests might reveal, it just seems kinder to not put an older person through this trauma.

K: So what choices do they have if they don't want to go to the hospital?

S: Many patients are able to receive appropriate pain control and treatment in their own familiar environment, whether in their own homes or a care facility. That would prevent traumatizing them by placing them in a hospital.

K: Is there an advance directive that would prohibit a person from being automatically hospitalized?

S: Yes. Individuals who prefer treatment in their own homes, or care facility, will need to fill out a Do Not Hospitalize Order. This medical directive eliminates any unnecessary hospitalization, yet it allows patients to be hospitalized after they, or the person who has been given authority to make medical decisions for them, have talked with the attending physician and hospitalization is deemed to be absolutely necessary. Then, and only then, would they be admitted to a hospital. A Do Not Hospitalize Order may be written by the patient's doctor and placed in her or his medical records. A copy also needs to be placed in the *Sandra Haymon Refrigerator Door Emergency Medical Information Kit*, otherwise known as the plastic pocket you put on the refrigerator door.

K: Put the information in there though. Don't leave it in the box, right?

S: Right! It's always a good idea to give copies of this order to family members who might be involved in making medical decisions. Of course, this is true for any medical directive. Hospitalization is a choice, as long as you make the decision in advance.

Do Not Hospitalize Order

I, _____, being over the legal age required by law and of sound mind do voluntarily and intentionally make known my desire and will that a **Do Not Hospitalize Order** be placed in my medical records. I direct that (1) I not be hospitalized (as provided by state law) for any condition for which I may receive the same type medical treatment in my own residence (home or care facility); (2) I not be subjected to diagnostic testing of possible illnesses or diseases for which treatment would not be expected to positively contribute to my quality of physical and mental life; (3) I am hospitalized only after the attending physician and I, or the attending physician and my health care surrogate deem hospitalization to be absolutely necessary for my comfort and/or pain control.

In the event I have a hopeless (not necessarily terminal in the legal sense) condition as determined by at least two licensed medical physicians (more if required by state law) who have personally examined me and determined there is no reasonable medical probability of my recovery from said condition to a meaningful quality of physical and mental life, I direct that my treatment be one of *comfort measures only* and that treatment be limited to pain management and comfort.

I fully understand I will only be hospitalized after the attending physician and I, or the attending physician and my health care surrogate have determined hospitalization to be absolutely necessary for my comfort and/or pain management. I fully understand that I may revoke this directive at any time. I understand the importance of this decision; I am competent to make this decision; and I voluntarily and freely sign this on (date) _____ in the presence of witnesses.

Patient: _____
(signature)

Print Name: _____

Address: _____

_____

Witness: _____   Witness: _____
(signature)   (signature)

Print Name: _____   Print Name: _____

Address: _____   Address: _____

_____   _____

Acknowledgment: Notarize if Required by State Law

State of _____)
)ss
County of _____)

On this date _____, before me personally appeared _____ ,
to me known to be the person described in and who executed the foregoing instrument and acknowledged to me
that (she/he) _____ executed the same as (her/his) _____ free act and deed.

_____   My commission expires: _____
Notary Public

© 1996 Magnolia Productions, Inc.

Feeding Tubes

K: Dr. Haymon, there is a lot of controversy about feeding tubes. Are there special considerations we should take into account when making a decision regarding feeding tubes where the elderly are concerned?

S: Kathryn, this is another heart-wrenching decision that has to be made on an individual basis. Once again, I am not trying to persuade people one way or the other. My intent is only to review different types of feeding tubes and discuss the pros and cons of this most difficult decision.

K: You say there are different types?

S: Yes, there are several ways to provide nutrition and medications artificially. One way is through nasogastric tubes. With this procedure, the tube is actually inserted into the person's nose, down through the esophagus and into the stomach. Another way is through gastrostomy tubes. These tubes are surgically inserted into the stomach wall. With both the nasogastric and the gastrostomy tubes, fluids can either be poured in or pumped in mechanically. The third means, and probably the one most familiar, is through a needle inserted into the patient's vein. This is commonly referred to as an IV. Technically, it is known as artificial intravenous hydration.

K: Is one procedure better than another?

S: Just as with CPR, there are certain risks associated with artificially feeding frail, elderly patients, no matter what procedure is used.

K: What are some of those risks?

S: Should the tube become displaced, or if regurgitated fluid enters the lungs, there is the risk of the person developing pneumonia. Also, ulcers and infections may result from certain feeding tubes. Agitated patients may have to be sedated or restrained in order to keep them from removing the tubes. Immobility is another problem because that often results in bed sores and their limbs becoming stiff. It is also common for patients on artificial feeding to get diarrhea, which may further increase the likelihood of bed sores. A really sad thing is that patients on feeding tubes often become more isolated, simply because there is less need for contact with caregivers. When an individual can still take in food and water by mouth, even if she or he has to be hand fed, there is interaction with other people at least three times a day when food is brought in. Well, that isn't the case when a person is being fed artificially. This isolation may be extremely difficult for some elderly individuals to tolerate. Many of them

> Should the tube become displaced, or if regurgitated fluid enters the lungs, there is the risk of the person developing pneumonia.

are already scared and afraid. Many don't even know where they are. This seems especially true for patients suffering from dementia. Besides these obvious risks, there is another factor which needs to be considered for patients who are coherent. Even though these patients are being fed artificially, they may perceive they are being allowed to starve because they are not being offered food. Many of them have reported that the smell of food causes them to experience the sensation of hunger, which is agonizing for them.

> ...frail, elderly people almost never regain the ability to take in food and water by mouth.

Kathryn, there is no question that thousands of patients' lives have been prolonged with artificial feeding, especially younger, healthier patients. However, frail, elderly people almost never regain the ability to take in food and water by mouth. In the United States today, there are approximately 10,000 patients in nursing homes and hospitals who are unable to make any purposeful response to their surroundings, and yet they are being maintained on feeding tubes.

K: I have heard withholding or withdrawing artificial feeding causes a painful death.

S: Pain control is a real concern. However, withholding artificial feeding results in dehydration before starvation. Consequently, pain and certain discomforts associated with starvation would probably not be experienced. The reported physical sensations that are present during dehydration are dry mouth and a sense of thirst. Furthermore, some research indicates there is a release of natural, pain-relieving chemicals as the body dehydrates. Consequently, pain the patient may be feeling from other illnesses, like cancer, actually might be lessened.

K: This is such a difficult topic, but I am also wondering if there are any other benefits besides the natural, pain-relieving chemicals associated with dehydration?

S: Yes. Without feeding tubes, frail, elderly patients may have the opportunity to die a more peaceful death because, as the person dehydrates, there is less fluid in the throat and lungs. Consequently, there would be less need for suctioning and less congestion, which might make it easier for them to breathe. Since fluids would not be continually pumped in, the patient would urinate less frequently and be less disposed to diarrhea, which might lessen the risk of bed sores.

K: Even with all of this information, however, there are still people who believe we should do absolutely everything we can — any heroic measure to keep people alive.

S: You're right. There are two sides to this coin. As with all controversial issues, there are always different ways of looking at the same question. Often these perspectives are diametrically opposed. On the one side of the coin there is the contention that food and water are basic human rights, and no matter what the chances of recovery, everything possible should be done to prolong life. On the other side of this same coin is the contention that artificially feeding a person does not prolong life but, in fact, prolongs the dying process and is much like using a respirator to force air into the lungs of the patient. In addition, the inability to take in fluids by mouth is viewed by many as a terminal medical condition. Their conviction is that withholding artificial feeding is to allow a natural death to occur.

K: Is there a general feeling or agreement among members of the medical community regarding feeding tubes?

S: Medical evidence is quite clear that dehydration in the end-stage of any terminal illness is a very compassionate and natural way to die.

K: Is our choice a limited yes or no regarding the feeding tubes?

S: Not always. In many states, people actually have several choices. They may choose to introduce a feeding tube when the patient can no longer take in fluids by mouth. They may also choose artificial feeding on a time-limited basis, or individuals may make conscious choices not to introduce artificial feeding at all. I encourage individuals to check with their doctors and find out what choices they have in their state. I also recommend that people talk with their doctors to find out how they feel about feeding tubes. Some physicians refuse to withhold feeding tubes. If the person's choice is not to introduce a feeding tube, but the doctor is of an entirely different opinion, then they will probably need to change doctors and find a physician who honors the patient's wishes, regardless of the doctor's personal opinion. It does seem, however, emotionally more difficult for some family members and physicians to withdraw a feeding tube, rather than to withhold it in the beginning. Once the tube is in place, it seems emotionally very difficult to make the decision to take it out. In fact, there are many medical doctors who are reluctant to withdraw a tube, once it has been introduced. Even when it was introduced on a time-limited basis, they are still reluctant to take it out. We can understand that. Not only does this have to do with moral issues, but there may be some legal implications in this. The important thing is to discuss these options with your medical provider. Discuss them with your loved ones and encourage them to make these decisions for themselves, in advance.

> Medical evidence is quite clear that dehydration in the end-stage of any terminal illness is a very compassionate and natural way to die.

Hospice and Comfort Measures Only

K: Dr. Haymon, where does the hospice approach fit in with these end-of-life medical decisions?

S: The hospice approach is one of comfort-measures-only. It was designed primarily for cancer patients. At this time, it might be helpful to review the three primary goals of medical treatment.

These goals are cure, stabilization, and comfort. When cure is the goal, the prescribed treatment is intended to cure the pathology, the illness. With the goal of stabilization, the intent of medical treatment is to stabilize the pathology. And, when comfort is the goal, it is often understood there is no cure and no means of stabilization. Therefore, the goal is to keep the person comfortable and to help prepare her or him for a natural and dignified death. This last goal is the goal of hospice programs. This is commonly referred to as a comfort-measures-only approach. The emphasis of this approach is on management of pain and other symptoms, and on quality of life, rather than on length of life. If the person opts for this approach, it does not mean we stop treating or caring for her or him. It simply means we allow her or him to die naturally, instead of prolonging the dying process.

> ...the goal is to keep the person comfortable and to help prepare her or him for a natural and dignified death.

K: What would be some of the comfort measures that could be provided?

S: Often, comfort measures include, but are not limited to, pain medication, medications to reduce fever, oxygen to make breathing easier, routine nursing care, such as keeping the patient clean and dry, and providing emotional and spiritual support.

K: Is medical treatment a choice or an option?

S: Certain medical treatments are optional. Radiation and chemotherapy would not be administered in an effort to cure, but might be used to relieve pain. Antibiotics would also be used to relieve pain, but not in an attempt to cure. Since cure and stabilization are normally ruled out, prior to opting for comfort-measures-only, there would be no need for diagnostic testing. Therefore, the person would be protected from any unnecessary, painful, invasive procedures. Feeding tubes would not be started. IV's would be used for pain medication, but not as a means of prolonging the dying process. Surgical procedures would be performed only if necessary to enhance the person's comfort.

K: Is there an advance directive for this choice?

S: Individuals for whom cure is not realistically possible, and who desire as high a quality of life as possible for the time they have remaining, may decide on the comfort-measures-only approach. In those cases, the patient or person responsible for making medical decisions would need to discuss this with the attending physician. A comfort-measures-only order is then placed in the patient's medical records.

K: Let me guess, a copy needs to be placed in the *Sandra Haymon Refrigerator Door Emergency Medical Information Kit*, otherwise known as the plastic envelope on the refrigerator door.

S: It is also important for individuals to give copies to those who may be called upon to make medical decisions for them.

K: I have heard that hospice programs may be very helpful. What services do they provide?

S: You're right, Kathryn, hospice programs offer an invaluable service. Primarily, they offer a team of professionals and specially-trained volunteers to address the medical, social, psychological and even spiritual needs of the patient. Should patients decide to stay in their own homes, a hospice team is often available 24 hours a day, 7 days a week, for support, consultation and visits.

For individuals who wish to remain in the nursing home or other care facility, the hospice team may become an adjunct to the staff, advising, teaching, observing, and providing extra equipment, as well as being supportive to the patient and family. In many communities, there are in-patient hospice facilities which incorporate the entire hospice philosophy into a unique setting with specially-trained staff.

Goals for the Last Days and Months of Life

K: It is very difficult to talk about death, or our last days, but that really is something we must talk about.

S: Kathryn, there are many reasonable goals for the last days and months of one's life. The alleviation of pain, the reconciliation of relationships, and joy — joy experienced in laughing about old times with friends and loved ones, looking at old photos, and celebrating one's life. Those are all meaningful goals. Also, having friends and relatives share in the grief, anger, and fear, as well as having an opportunity to say goodbye, seem to be worthwhile goals that may bring comfort and closure for the individual, as well as for family members and friends.

...there are many reasonable goals for the last days and months of one's life.

CHAPTER 4

ADVANCE DIRECTIVES

K: Dr. Haymon, are there other advance directives we need to be aware of? Could you recap the ones we've already talked about?

S: Yes, I'd love to, but first let me state that I am not an attorney, nor am I giving legal advice. The information I share with you stems from my own personal experience and my own understanding of these issues. I would also remind people, not only do laws differ from state to state, but state laws change. Therefore, I highly recommend that individuals *check with an attorney* in their state to make certain these documents are appropriate.

Living Wills

See sample form on pages 48–49.

We talked about living wills and most states have now passed a Natural Death Act. Some states refer to this as a Health-Care Decisions Act, which provides for living will declarations. In most states, this document must be prepared while the person is competent, and in most states the person's signature has to be witnessed. As I mentioned earlier, most living wills only address the issue of artificial life support, so individuals who do not want to be placed on artificial life support, when there is no hope of them recovering, might consider a living will. However, I want to remind people that a living will is not effective until it's delivered to their health-care provider.

K: You say the primary purpose of living wills is to prohibit the use of artificial life support, but could the person include other wishes in this document?

S: Yes. There are a number of things a person might include in her or his living will. She or he might want to name a person to carry out their wishes, should they become unable to. And here's another thing about living wills; they don't necessarily prohibit the use of all life-prolonging procedures. Individuals may want to specify particular procedures to be used, when those procedures are to be withheld, and when they're to be withdrawn. They might also want to address other issues, should they become terminally ill. For example, what role will their religious preferences play in their care decisions. Those wishes could be included in a living will.

K: **What if a person fills out a living will and then later changes her or his mind?**

S: It's important to make a note of everybody you've given a copy of your living will to, so if you should change your mind, and want to amend it or revoke it, you can recover all copies.

K: **Are most living wills fairly straightforward?**

S: Usually they are, however, as with most legal documents, there can be problems with living wills. So if you have any reason for concern, you should seek advice from your attorney. For example, living wills must be understood by the patient, as well as the physician.

K: **What other kinds of problems come up?**

S: Some common questions in regard to a living will are: What's considered artificial? What constitutes a terminal condition? What defines a life-prolonging procedure? Who determines when there's no hope of recovery? The point here is, due to the possibility of misinterpretation, it is extremely important that living wills be explicit and leave as little room for subjective interpretation as possible.

K: **Dr. Haymon, what if a person has a living will and then becomes unable to make decisions for her or himself, but their family believes differently? Can family members override a living will?**

S: Not normally, except that under certain circumstances, as may be set forth by state law, one's family should not be able to override a living will. The whole purpose of making these decisions for yourself in advance is to ensure your wishes are carried out—not your family's wishes.

K: **You said earlier that individuals may change their living wills. What if they simply don't want them anymore?**

S: People who are competent may revoke their living wills in a number of ways. They may physically destroy their living will by tearing it up. They just need to be sure they destroy all copies. They may also orally state their intent to revoke their living will in the presence of witnesses. This situation might occur while they're in the hospital. Maybe they don't have their living will right there with them, but at the last minute they say, "No, no, I changed my mind." If they're competent when they state that, and they have a couple of witnesses, their living will is revoked at that time. Another way is to write "revoked" on the face of their living will. But once again, all copies need to be treated the same. They may also write their intentions to revoke their living will, date, and sign the form, and get a couple of people to witness their signature. Living wills are also revoked by means of a subsequently executed living will that materially differs from the preceding one. If you write out a living will today, and later decide you want to make significant changes to it, then the new living will takes precedence over the old one.

Health Care Surrogate   *See sample form on page 50.*

K: Dr. Haymon, I've heard a term I'm not familiar with—health care surrogate. Tell us about health care surrogates, if you please.

S: As with other legal documents, state laws may differ, but in many states competent individuals may name a health care surrogate to make medical decisions for them, in the event that they become incompetent or incapable of making their own informed decisions. Normally, this document must be in writing and signed by two witnesses. In many states, only one witness may be the spouse or a blood relative. Customarily, the named surrogate may not be one of the witnesses.

K: Are there special requirements in order to be named a health care surrogate?

S: Not normally. Customarily, any competent adult may be named health care surrogate. However, some states require the named surrogate to agree in writing to accept those responsibilities.

K: When would a surrogate need to take over?

S: Surrogate directives usually become effective only when the attending physician determines the patient no longer has the capacity to make informed decisions and give informed consent. Here's a side note: Usually a judge is not needed to declare an individual legally incompetent to make medical decisions, however, most states require the patient be examined by two physicians to determine capacity. The results of these examinations are then placed in the patient's medical records.

K: So what would a surrogate caregiver be expected to do?

S: The functions of health care surrogates also differ from state to state. In some states, health care surrogates may do a number of things. They might be able to review the patient's medical records, consult with the patient's doctor, give medical consent for treatment, apply for medical benefits on behalf of the patient, and exercise other rights set forth by state law.

K: There are things a surrogate caregiver is not allowed to do?

S: Yes. Many states prohibit certain functions of healthcare surrogates. For example, in some states, the healthcare surrogate is prohibited from giving consent to electroshock, sterilization, psychosurgery, or voluntary admission to a mental hospital. Sometimes they're prohibited from giving consent to experimental treatment.

K: If the person, or patient, gets better and can handle her or his own affairs, what happens then?

S: Should the individual regain competency, the healthcare surrogate would then cease to act on behalf of that person. However, I strongly recommend you check with an attorney in your state in order to gain accurate information to any questions you might have regarding healthcare surrogates.

Health Care Proxy

K: This may be the worst of situations, but what if a person becomes unable to make her or his own decisions, there are no advance directives, and they have not named a health care surrogate? What would happen then?

S: Unfortunately, this situation occurs quite frequently.

K: Is that because people just don't plan ahead?

S: Well, that's the obvious answer. But at an even deeper level, many elderly people are not even aware they have all these choices. People who are 75, 80, or 90 years old, grew up long before we even had CPR. The medical technology we have today was not available then. The good news is, some states have provisions for the situation you described. In the event a resident in a health-care facility has not named a health care surrogate, or maybe a surrogate has been named, but for some reason can't act on behalf of the individual, then a health care proxy may be named. In this case, the facility would find a competent person willing to act on behalf of the patient as the health care proxy. However, many state laws require health care proxies be appointed from a priority list.

K: Who would be on that list?

S: Kathryn, let me say again that state laws are different. So the priority list for health care proxies may, or may not, follow this order. But customarily, the first person on the list would be a judicially appointed guardian of the patient, who's been authorized to consent to medical treatment on behalf of the patient, that is if a guardian has been appointed. Next would be the patient's competent spouse. Third would be the competent adult child of the patient, or a majority of competent adult children who are reasonably available. Next might be a competent parent of the patient.

K: If we're talking about elderly people, their parents probably wouldn't be an option would they?

S: Probably not in most cases. However, some people who are in their sixties and maybe even those in their seventies still have parents who are living. Sometimes the parents are in better health than their children.

K: I hadn't really thought about that.

S: And lastly, if none of these people are available, a competent adult relative who has exhibited special care and concern for the patient might be appointed, or perhaps a competent friend of the patient.

K: You told us earlier that a health care surrogate normally has to agree to accept these responsibilities. Is that also true of the health care proxy?

S: Yes. Usually the proxy is notified in writing and normally proxies must also convey their agreement in writing.

K: Why would a health care surrogate not agree? Maybe walk me through a situation, so I can better understand.

S: Okay. Let's use you as an example. Let's say you decide you want to name your sister as your health care surrogate, or perhaps she is chosen as your health care proxy. Yet, nobody has even asked her if she would be willing to do that. Then let's say you're in an automobile accident and you're comatose. Someone from the hospital calls your sister and starts asking her all sorts of questions—whether you are to be placed on a respirator; whether CPR is to be administered if necessary; whether you have advance directives; who will pay for your care? They ask her all these questions. And she says, "Well, excuse me, nobody even asked me if I would be willing to make these decisions. The truth is, I don't want this responsibility. Call somebody else." So you see, when we think about naming somebody to make these medical decisions for us, it's very important we talk to them about it and give them the opportunity to either accept or reject this responsibility.

K: So that's another choice then—who carries out these decisions for you, even though you may have filled out advance directives ahead of time?

S: Once the health care proxy agrees to accept this responsibility on behalf of the person, then she or he must comply with the provisions of the surrogate law for that particular state. Health care proxies, as well as health care surrogates, are required to make healthcare decisions they believe the person would make for herself or himself. Furthermore, should the decision to be made involve life-prolonging procedures, most health care facilities require the surrogate or proxy to show clear and convincing evidence of the patient's wishes.

K: How could you prove that?

S: Well, normally, valid living wills are accepted as standard of proof. However, each case is determined upon it's particular circumstances. Once again, and I know I've said this three or four times, state laws differ. I'm not an attorney, and I'm not trying to give legal advice here, I just want people to be aware of these issues. I urge individuals to check with an attorney in their state, should they have questions about this.

K: That certainly seems fair enough.

Guardians

K: Let's talk about guardians for a minute. You stated that one of the first people to be appointed as a health care proxy would be a guardian. Do we need to know more about guardianship as well?

S: There are situations where a guardian may be appointed. However, these situations tend to be very complex and must be handled on an individual basis. So people need to contact an attorney in the event they believe they need a guardian for their loved one. But I will tell you this, a guardian is someone who has been appointed to handle a person's affairs. Guardians may be given full power to make all decisions for the individual. They may be given power just over the person, or just over the person's property, or any combination of these. Or they may only be allowed to make emergency medical decisions for the person. Though most states provide for the same types of guardianship, there are specific laws pertaining to these provisions and filing must be done by an attorney.

Durable Power of Attorney *See sample form on page 51.*

K: **A friend of mine has a durable power of attorney for her mother and it sounds very complicated. Could you talk to us briefly about durable power of attorney?**

S: Yes, Kathryn. In most states, a durable power of attorney specifies exactly the powers the patient is giving to the person holding the power—their agent. Power may include consent to an arrangement for a number of things. For example, agents may be given power to make medical decisions for the person. They may be given power to make therapeutical and surgical decisions. They may be able to decide which drugs would be administered. They also might be able to transfer property for the person, or borrow money, or even manage bank accounts. There's any number of specific or general powers the person holding durable power of attorney may have.

K: **Who can hold this durable power of attorney?**

S: Customarily, any competent adult named by the person to act as her or his agent may hold durable power of attorney in those states which have such provisions. If the person is a relative, this customarily has to be stated. The person holding the power of attorney cannot delegate that authority to another person. Also, just as with surrogate caregivers and health care proxies, persons holding power of attorney must attempt to carry out the patient's wishes.

K: **This is a complicated question to me. Does a durable power of attorney remain effective, should the patient become mentally incapacitated?**

S: Not unless that's stated. Should a petition be filed to determine the patient's mental capacity, the durable power of attorney is normally suspended at that time. However, in some states the durable power of attorney may remain effective, should the patient become functionally incompetent, but I'm told this must include language which clearly states the power is not affected by the individual's mental disability, except as provided by statute. I want to emphasize the importance of your attorney wording this document to communicate clearly the intent of the patient to this effect. When so worded, the durable power of attorney would then give the designated person — the agent— authority to make healthcare decisions, or perhaps other decisions on behalf of the patient, should she or he become incapacitated, until and unless, a guardianship is created. Then those legal provisions would apply.

K: Could a person delegate power to just make medical decisions?

S: Yes, in some states. In this case, the designated person is only authorized to make medical decisions on behalf of the patient.

K: When would a durable power of attorney expire?

S: I'm sure you're tired of hearing this, but state laws differ.

K: Great, just when we needed a universal law!

S: Normally a durable power of attorney expires in three ways. It expires, of course, at the death of the patient. It would expire at the time the patient revoked the power. It would also expire if the patient is adjudicated incompetent by a court of law, unless otherwise stated in the durable power of attorney.

K: So do I hear you saying you need an attorney to fill out a durable power of attorney?

S: In some states you may have to, but in many states there are standard forms.

Case Law

K: Dr. Haymon, what if the person has no advance directives and no one has been appointed to make medical decisions for her or him? Then what happens?

S: In the event the patient has not initiated any of the documents that I've discussed, and no guardian has been appointed, there are methods which an attorney might use to assist in carrying out the patient's wishes. This is very risky. I would admonish individuals not to rely on their understanding of case law in any state, unless of course they are attorneys. In fact, the courts may have altered a portion of the law which affects this decision, even the night before. It may be important that someone in your family, or some friend, understand the legal issues and discuss this matter with a private attorney in the event the patient has no advance directives and no agent has been named.

General Discussion

K: Dr. Haymon, thank you for helping us understand more about advance directives and these many legal issues. You've really taken some complicated material and presented it in a way that most of us can understand. But now could we talk just for a

minute? This is so complicated, and I have some simple questions. For instance, here you talk about living wills. Is that different from a last will and testament?

S: Absolutely. A last will and testament addresses issues to be handled after the person has died. A living will addresses issues while the person is still living.

K: Would it be a comparison to make, for instance, between an executor of an estate and a guardian?

S: Yes, if you're asked to handle a person's estate and make decisions after the person has died, then you're primarily dealing with real property, bank accounts, and other legal issues. However, if you're a guardian for that person, you will be making decisions that will affect the person while she or he is living.

K: Regarding the end-of-life decisions, or advance directives we've talked about, I feel so much more aware now, but if I were to call my mother tomorrow, my 88-year-old mother, and say, "Mother, you need to do this, this, and this," I'm not quite sure yet what those things are. Dr. Haymon, what should I tell my mother she needs to do? Can you summarize that for me?

S: I guess we're going to assume that she doesn't have any forms, any documents, or advance directives. We'll just assume she has done nothing, right?

K: She's got her last will and testament and she's appointed my sister as the executrix of her estate. She thinks she's done everything she needs to do.

S: Okay, then first of all, you'll need to talk with her about the choices she has. She's 88 years old. She probably doesn't even know she has a choice about CPR, or a choice as to whether she will be treated in a hospital. She may know a little about living wills, but she may not understand that in a living will she may specify any number of wishes. Kathryn, your job would be to talk with her. You might say, "Mother, I was listening to some tapes the other day (or reading this book), and Dr. Haymon said we have a choice about CPR." Talk with her about her choices, then give her an opportunity to think about them. I wouldn't ask her to fill out any forms that day. This is a lot to take in. So you might not want to talk with her about all of her choices at one time. But do talk with her and help her come to some understanding about how she feels about certain choices. After you've talked with her, and she understands her choices, then encourage her to fill out a living will and other advance directives.

K: Could I get a basic form for her and then fill in the other things she might want?

S: Yes. Most states have standard forms for living wills. You can find those at office supply stores or a doctor's office. There's also one in the Emergency Kit included with this book. These are very basic forms. It's fill in the blanks. The only caution is to be sure that there are two witnesses to the signature and get it notarized, if that is required in the state in which she lives.

K: It can't be me? It could be her neighbor? It could be someone else? But I can't serve as one of the witnesses?

S: In some states you can, unless you are the named health care surrogate. Let me give you an example: In the state of Florida, the living wills my mother and stepfather filled out provided a section where they could name surrogate caregivers. There was also a section for the surrogates to sign accepting responsibility of surrogate caregiver. It differs from state to state, but most states have standard forms. If it has a place for a surrogate caregiver at the bottom, which I think most of them do now, that eliminates an additional form.

K: Could she hand write on the bottom of her living will, "I do not want to be resuscitated with CPR," or is that the second form?

S: She probably could do that. Most living wills can be tailored to fit most needs. So she probably could write that in, but she would need to write it above her signature and above the witnesses' signatures. You don't want it to look like somebody just added that in. You asked if a surrogate caregiver could be a witness. In some states you can, and in some states you can't. I'll tell you what happened to me. My parents had filled out their living wills and I signed as one of the witnesses. Then one of the nurses at the hospital signed, and thank goodness she also caught our mistake and said, "Oh, no, Dr. Haymon, you can't witness this, you're the named surrogate." So we left my signature, but then we got a third person to be one of the witnesses.

K: So I'm hearing that we can take care of this relatively easily if we listen to these tapes or read your book and find out what we're looking for. If I call Mother and say, "Dr. Haymon says we need a guardian, a surrogate caregiver, and you've got my sister as executrix of the estate," can one person serve as all of the things you said are needed?

S: Yes, there can be just one person. You will need to be sure, though, that you have the appropriate documents to cover all that. One of the recommendations, and here again, I am not giving legal advice, so if my attorney is out there listening, I am not giving legal advice. Okay…

K: We're just asking you to be a friend — someone who has been through it. And I think we have qualified that.

S: Well, one of the documents I might recommend would be a durable power of attorney. Specify in that power of attorney all of the things you want the named person to have the authority to do — make legal decisions for you, medical decisions, and even life-prolonging decisions. Remember, these have to be specifically written in. Also be sure that person is willing to accept this responsibility. Get her or him to sign, stating she or he agrees to perform these duties.

K: One thing that really touched me in your discussion of this legalese, if you will, was when you pointed out that if you're going to give someone this responsibility

you really need to tell them, verbally, what your choices are, and not give them that responsibility lightly. Have you done that for yourself? Do you have all these things signed? Have you appointed someone to make the decisions on heroic measures for you? And should we, as younger women, complete these forms?

S: Yes. I encourage everybody to make these choices for themselves. These are not issues that just deal with old age. God forbid, I could have an accident as I leave here. Yes, I do have these forms filled out and I have named one of my sisters to be my surrogate caregiver. We have talked about all these issues and she has agreed to be willing to make the decisions she feels I would make, if I were competent to make them for myself. But the bottom line here is, all of us need to go ahead and make our decisions in advance. This is not just about being elderly.

K: Well I, for one, thank you, because I'm so much better informed now. I do really commend you, Dr. Haymon, for sharing your story. Thank you.

FORMS

**The following pages contain reproductions of several forms supplied to you in the Sandra Haymon Refrigerator Door Emergency Information Kit.
Take a moment to review each one.**

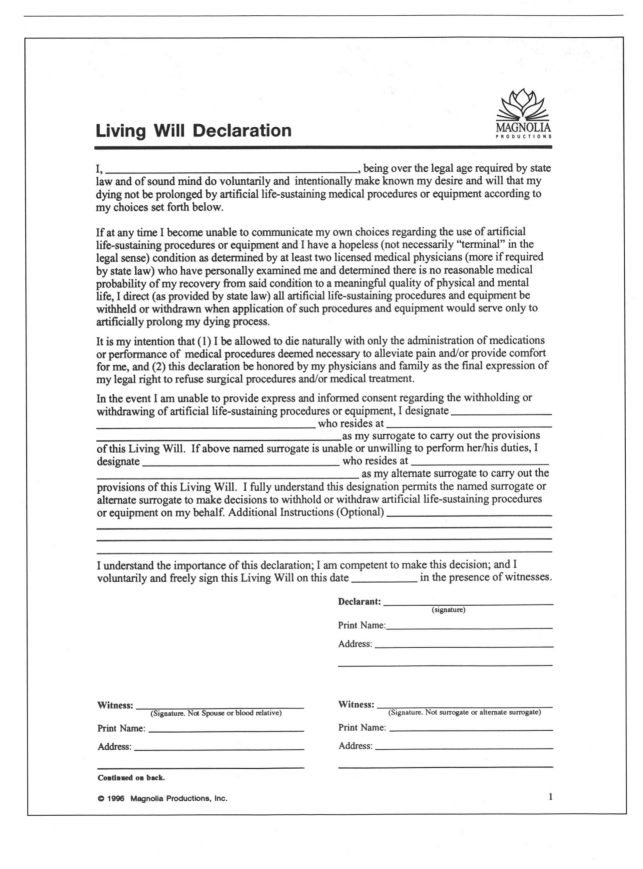

Living Will Declaration

I, _____, being over the legal age required by state
law and of sound mind do voluntarily and intentionally make known my desire and will that my
dying not be prolonged by artificial life-sustaining medical procedures or equipment according to
my choices set forth below.

If at any time I become unable to communicate my own choices regarding the use of artificial
life-sustaining procedures or equipment and I have a hopeless (not necessarily "terminal" in the
legal sense) condition as determined by at least two licensed medical physicians (more if required
by state law) who have personally examined me and determined there is no reasonable medical
probability of my recovery from said condition to a meaningful quality of physical and mental
life, I direct (as provided by state law) all artificial life-sustaining procedures and equipment be
withheld or withdrawn when application of such procedures and equipment would serve only to
artificially prolong my dying process.

It is my intention that (1) I be allowed to die naturally with only the administration of medications
or performance of medical procedures deemed necessary to alleviate pain and/or provide comfort
for me, and (2) this declaration be honored by my physicians and family as the final expression of
my legal right to refuse surgical procedures and/or medical treatment.

In the event I am unable to provide express and informed consent regarding the withholding or
withdrawing of artificial life-sustaining procedures or equipment, I designate _____
_____ who resides at _____
_____ as my surrogate to carry out the provisions
of this Living Will. If above named surrogate is unable or unwilling to perform her/his duties, I
designate _____ who resides at _____
_____ as my alternate surrogate to carry out the
provisions of this Living Will. I fully understand this designation permits the named surrogate or
alternate surrogate to make decisions to withhold or withdraw artificial life-sustaining procedures
or equipment on my behalf. Additional Instructions (Optional) _____
_____
_____
_____

I understand the importance of this declaration; I am competent to make this decision; and I
voluntarily and freely sign this Living Will on this date _____ in the presence of witnesses.

Declarant: _____
                         (signature)

Print Name: _____

Address: _____

_____

Witness: _____
              (Signature. Not Spouse or blood relative)

Print Name: _____

Address: _____

_____

Witness: _____
              (Signature. Not surrogate or alternate surrogate)

Print Name: _____

Address: _____

_____

Continued on back.

1

Acceptance of Surrogate Designation

I, _____ , do hereby accept responsibility to act as surrogate
on behalf of _____ should she/he become incapacitated.

Surrogate: _____
(Signature)

Print Name: _____

Address: _____

_____

Witness: _____
(Signature)

Print Name: _____

Address: _____

_____

Witness: _____
(Signature)

Print Name: _____

Address: _____

_____

Acceptance of Alternate Surrogate Designation

I, _____ , do hereby accept responsibility to act as alternate
surrogate on behalf of _____ should she/he become incapacitated.

Alternate Surrogate: _____
(Signature)

Print Name: _____

Address: _____

_____

Witness: _____
(Signature)

Print Name: _____

Address: _____

_____

Witness: _____
(Signature)

Print Name: _____

Address: _____

_____

Acknowledgment: Notarize if Required by State Law

State of _____)
County of _____)ss

On this date _____, before me personally appeared _____ ,
to me known to be the person described in and who executed the foregoing instrument and acknowledged to me
that (she/he) _____ executed the same as (her/his) _____ free act and deed.

_____   My commission expires: _____
Notary Public

© 1996 Magnolia Productions, Inc.   2

Health Care
Surrogate Designation

In the event I am unable to provide express and informed consent for medical treatment, diagnostic and/or surgical procedures, I, _____ , designate _____ , who resides at _____ _____ as my surrogate for health care decisions. If above named surrogate is unable or unwilling to perform her/his duties, I designate _____ _____ , who resides at _____ _____ as my alternate surrogate for health care decisions. I fully understand this designation permits the named surrogate or alternate surrogate to make health care decisions and to provide, withhold, or withdraw consent on my behalf; to apply for public benefits; and to authorize my admission to/from health care facilities.

Additional instructions (optional) _____ _____

Declarant: _____
            (Signature)

Print Name: _____

Address: _____

_____

Witness: _____
         (Signature. Not surrogate or alternate surrogate)

Print Name: _____

Address: _____

Witness: _____
         (Signature. Not surrogate or alternate surrogate)

Print Name: _____

Address: _____

Acceptance of Surrogate Designation

I, _____ , do hereby accept responsibility to act as surrogate

on behalf of _____ should she/he become incapacitated.

Surrogate: _____
           (Signature)

Print Name: _____

Address: _____

_____

Acceptance of Alternate Surrogate Designation

I, _____ , do hereby accept responsibility to act as alternate

surrogate on behalf of _____ should she/he become incapacitated.

Alternate
Surrogate: _____
           (Signature)

Print Name: _____

Address: _____

_____

Acknowledgment: Notarize if Required by State Law

State of _____)
)ss
County of _____)

On this date _____, before me personally appeared _____ ,
to me known to be the person described in and who executed the foregoing instrument and acknowledged to me
that (she/he) _____ executed the same as (her/his) _____ free act and deed.

_____   My commission expires: _____
        Notary Public

Durable Power of Attorney

MAGNOLIA
PRODUCTIONS

I, _____ , *(Principal)* being over the legal age required by state law and of sound mind do voluntarily and intentionally designate and appoint _____ , *(Agent)*, who resides at _____ as the sole agent to act on my behalf in the event I am unable to make and communicate my own decisions regarding my health and medical treatment. If above named Agent is unable or unwilling to perform her/his duties, I designate _____ , who resides at _____ , my alternate agent. This power and authority shall become effective only after two licensed medical physicians (more if required by law) have personally examined me and certified that I do not have the mental capacity to make informed decisions and give informed consent.

I delegate to my Agent authority to make decisions on my behalf in arranging for and consenting to medical evaluations, medical treatment, surgical procedures, and the administration of drugs and other pharmaceutical substances. This delegation shall include authority to make arrangements on my behalf and consent to medical hospitalization, psychiatric hospitalization, admission to nursing home or other care facility and/or hospice. My agent shall have authority to employ, replace, obtain reassignment, and/or discharge health care personnel to include medical physicians, nurses, dentists, psychiatrists, psychologists, physical therapists, or any other persons involved in my health care and treatment. My agent shall have the authority to visit me in any health care facility and/or transport me to any facility in any state for health care or treatment.

This delegation shall include authority to procure medical treatment on my behalf through the use of my personal assets and/or the sale of my real and/or personal properties. In the event an emergency should arise between such time a petition is filed and an adjudication is made concerning my capacity, my agent may petition the courts for permission to exercise the powers and authority delegated to my agent in this declaration of *Durable Power of Attorney*. Additional instructions (Optional):_____ _____

I understand that I may revoke this *Durable Power of Attorney* at any time. I fully understand the importance of this decision; I am competent to make this decision; and I voluntarily and freely sign this *Durable Power of Attorney* on this date _____ in the presence of witnesses.

Principal: _____   **Agent:** _____
Print Name: _____   Print Name: _____
Address: _____   Address: _____
_____   _____

         Alternate Agent: _____
         Print Name: _____
         Address: _____
         _____

Witness: _____   **Witness:** _____
Print Name: _____   Print Name: _____
Address _____   Address:_____
_____   _____

Acknowledgment: Notarize if Required by State Law

State of _____)
)ss
County of _____)

On this date _____ , before me personally appeared _____ , to me known to be the person described in and who executed the foregoing instrument and acknowledged to me that (she/he) _____ executed the same as (her/his) _____ free act and deed.

_____   My commission expires: _____
      Notary Public

Medical Information Release

MAGNOLIA
PRODUCTIONS

To: _____ ;   Date: _____
            (Medical Provider)

Address: _____

I authorize the above provider to release medical information regarding

_____   _____
   (Patient's first name & middle initial)   (Patient's last name)

SSN: _____ – _____ – _____   to: _____
     (Patient's Social Security Number)   (Provider's name – please print)

located at _____

The following information may be released. (Please initial and date all appropriate categories)

Information pertaining to HIV/AIDS diagnosis/treatment   _____   _____
                                                            (initials)   (date)

Information pertaining to drug/alcohol diagnosis/treatment   _____   _____
                                                               (initials)   (date)

Information pertaining to mental health diagnosis/treatment   _____   _____
                                                                (initials)   (date)

Information pertaining to all other medical diagnosis/treatment   _____   _____
                                                                    (initials)   (date)

This authorization automatically expires _____ months from _____ unless
                                           (# of months)   (today's date)
otherwise revoked prior to that date.

_____   OR   _____
     (Patient's signature)   (Signature of person authorized to make medical decisions for patient)

Print Name: _____   Print Name: _____

Address: _____   Address: _____

_____   _____

Phone: _____   Phone: _____

Acknowledgment: Notarize if Required by State Law

State of _____)
)ss
County of _____)

On this date _____, before me personally appeared _____ ,
to me known to be the person described in and who executed the foregoing instrument and acknowledged to me
that (she/he) _____ executed the same as (her/his) _____ free act and deed.

_____   My commission expires: _____
        Notary Public

© 1996 Magnolia Productions, Inc.

CHAPTER 5

LIVING ARRANGEMENTS

K: Dr. Haymon, when the time comes that our parents really need our help, what should we do?

S: For those of you who live in the same town with your parents, family companionship may be all they need in order to feel supported. However, your responsibilities may require you to do a number of other things in addition to regular phone calls and visits. You may have to help them with their grocery shopping or meal preparation. You may have to help them with their laundry, or do it for them. There may be yard work you need to help them with. Sometimes you may need to make some minor house repairs. You may need to help them pay their bills, make medical appointments, or complete insurance and Medicare forms, which seems to be an endless job. You may need to help with their medications. Remember the problems I had with my folks regarding medications? There are many things that may require your time and attention, so if you are able to hire others to do some of these things, if you can afford that, or if your parents can afford to, then I highly recommend it.

K: I was intrigued with the ingenuity you used for the pill problem. The fact was, they couldn't keep track of the pills. Were there any other little things you did cleverly around their home to make it more comfortable for them?

S: One of the things that comes to mind is that we had a problem with lights. I replaced a number of their lights with touch-on lamps. Most people are probably familiar with those. You can get them at Wal-Mart, K-Mart — any number of stores. Instead of having an on and off switch, it is designed so that they may touch the lamp anywhere on the metal part and the light comes on. It also accommodates three-way bulbs. I understand that now there are adapters which make any lamp a touch-on. I'm not sure they had those when I was going through this process. These adapters screw down into the socket of the lamp, then you put the bulb in. You can convert any lamp to a touch-on lamp. Having touch-on lights was very helpful for them. If they needed to get up and use the restroom in the middle of the night, or when they got up in the mornings — these people would get up before daylight — they could just reach over and touch the lamp and the light would come on. They wouldn't have to try to figure out how to turn it on. Plus my mother has arthritis, so turning on lamps was difficult for her. These lamps are also helpful for people who can't see well without their glasses. It enables people to have light in order to find their glasses. Another thing I had to do was in reference to their telephone. I bought a phone for them that had very large numbers on it. These phones are inexpensive and can be found at most large chain stores. Not only did it have large numbers, but I could program several phone numbers. All my folks had to do was to press one button to get 911, another button to reach me at work, and another to reach me at home. Right by the phone I put a large sheet of paper identifying the buttons. For example, button number one equaled 911; button number two equaled Sandra at home, etc., so they could dial the most frequently called numbers by just touching one button.

K: But you actually programmed it for them. You didn't just give them the phone and say, "Here, do this?"

S: Yes, I *had* to program it for them. My parents don't understand how to use a lot of new technology. Also, since they are hard of hearing, I purchased an amplifier to make the ringer on their telephone very, very loud. I think I got this at Radio Shack. It was only about $9.00. Later, I also had to put an adapter on their phone, so not only was the ringer loud, but a little light bulb would flash on and off, and they would know when their phone was ringing. Another thing they were having problems with was the remote control for their television set. They would be watching their favorite television program, and maybe they wanted to turn the volume up. However, they would touch the wrong button. Then they would go to another channel and couldn't get back to their program, so they would miss the end of their show. I bought a remote control with large buttons. Well, that didn't solve the problem. On the right side of this particular remote control were buttons for the power, volume, and for changing the channel up or down. All the other buttons were on the left side of the remote. So I got some tape, just plain white tape, and I taped the entire left side. I just wrapped the tape around and around the remote control. Then all they could do was turn their set on and off, increase or decrease the volume, and change the channels up or down. This significantly reduced the probabilities of them losing their channel.

> Actually, a trained person comes to the home and provides assistance with bathing, preparing meals, light house-keeping, minor medical services and companionship.

K: That's a great idea. You had to be creative. It almost sounds like you were grandma- and grandpa-proofing the house — similar to child-proofing. It sounds like it made a difference, made them more comfortable.

S: Kathryn, you do learn to be very creative, and all of these things take a lot of time. They also take a lot of energy. As I mentioned earlier, if you can hire somebody to do some of the yard work or house cleaning, by all means do so, but sometimes families just cannot afford this. In those cases, I would recommend talking to your parents' doctor and asking her or him to make a referral so they might receive some assistance.

K: I didn't realize there is that kind of assistance. Are you saying there are agencies where you can hire people to help with day-to-day chores?

S: There are many programs that provide homemaker and health services. Actually, a trained person comes to the home and provides assistance with bathing, preparing meals, light housekeeping, minor medical services and companionship. Some will also provide transportation to take them to and from shopping and medical appointments. There are also programs which provide transportation to community centers, where elderly individuals may go several times a week for meals and other social activities. However, depending on the person's level of functioning, you might want to contact an organization that actually brings meals to their home. I actually went through all this with my parents. The main thing is to help elderly people remain in their own homes for as long as they are able to, and for as long as they want to. Many of these programs allow elderly people to stay in their own homes for years.

K: Do most states have these organizations? Where would you find telephone numbers for them?

S: Yes. Most states have toll-free help lines which provide information, as well as referral services. These phone numbers are usually listed under Elder Affairs in the white pages of the telephone directory. Besides state agencies, there are other resources that might be able to help. For example, many churches and synagogues, as well as civic organizations and some social groups, offer similar assistance through volunteers. So for people who really can't afford to hire someone to come and help them, I would recommend they contact these agencies. Also, the American Association of Retired Persons (AARP) provides an invaluable amount of information. Because the need for assistance in caring for elderly people has become so great, there are a number of public and private companies that have begun to develop local and national care manager programs. In many states, elder care divisions have programs that provide case assessment, as well as case management, which also includes some placement services. Some states presently offer Medicaid-waiver programs that enable elderly individuals who are disabled to continue living at home by providing nursing home-level care (Medicaid will not normally pay for custodial care). However, when elderly people are enabled to stay in their own homes, it not only delays the loss of independence for them, but it also delays the need for a much more

> Many of these programs allow elderly people to stay in their own homes for years.

costly care program. I am told that under a federal pilot program, at least 12 states have now started programs for care managers — to guide caregivers through this maze of medical and social services.

K: Are there private companies that offer help, or is it primarily through state programs?

S: Kathryn, there are hundreds of private companies and their charges range anywhere from $10 to $85 per hour. It just depends on what you hire them to do. Corporations are gradually recognizing that, like child care, elder care really is a corporate issue because it affects absenteeism, as well as performance. Sometimes, when people are at work and they are worried about their mothers or fathers, they have to take time off and go to their homes. I know this from personal experience. It really can interfere with one's job. To address this, some corporations have already started a lot of programs which include seminars, support groups and telephone help lines. Most companies now have employee assistance programs, and a few companies provide elder/adult day care. I was just thrilled when I learned a number of companies are moving in that direction. I think, within the next decade, we are going to see more and more companies providing that for people. Some people may not be familiar with it, but we do have a Family Leave Act that was passed, I believe, in 1992. It allows individuals to take leave time from their jobs to care for their family members without having to worry about losing their jobs. They are guaranteed to have their jobs when they return, but there are certain criteria which must be met. So I would recommend that individuals either refer to the Act itself, or seek professional advice before they apply for this leave. Most companies would have a copy of this Family Leave Act in their personnel office or legal department.

> It allows individuals to take leave time from their jobs to care for their family members without having to worry about losing their jobs.

K: That's great to know. I have read that home-healthcare is becoming more and more popular.

S: Oh, it is. Within the past decade, more than 4,000 new home-healthcare agencies have opened. Since the shift appears to be away from expensive institutional care, the entire home-healthcare industry is expected to really expand because it is much less costly.

K: But what about those of us who live in one part of the country, and our parents live in another? I think we are called scattered families.

S: There are many companies that will find a care manager to actually take care of your parents for you. These care managers will serve as advocate, counselor, coordinator and/or liaison. They will also monitor other services your parents may need in order for them to stay in their own home. As you can see, Kathryn, there are many resources that provide help to enable elderly citizens to stay in their homes for as long as they are able to and want to.

K: That sounds great, but I wouldn't even know where to start. Would you just look in the yellow pages under *caregiver*? Where would you find a company like that?

S: You could start by calling Elder Care, which is usually listed in the white pages of the telephone directory. I have also included phone numbers. (Please see Resources, pages 135–157.)

K: What if elderly parents need more than just daily assistance?

S: Well, besides assistance programs, there is also the option of hiring someone to actually move into their homes to help care for them. This is usually quite expensive, and finding someone they would be compatible with — somebody that you trust — is often difficult, but you do have that option. There are certain companies that also provide assisted-living services, but they charge anywhere from $1,500 to $2,500 a month.

K: Dr. Haymon, forgive me, but I am still unclear as to what you would call a company that would provide this type of assistance.

S: Kathryn, this type of assistance is normally handled by home-healthcare agencies. So if you look in the yellow pages, under *Home-Healthcare,* usually you will find several of them listed.

K: Great, thank you. Let's face it, at some point, unless they die first, there will come a time when elderly people can no longer stay in their homes. What then?

S: That is true, and more often than not, other people recognize when that time comes long before the elderly person does. At that time, somebody has to make a decision as to where the elderly person is going to live. Usually, this is a very difficult decision.

K: So, many people have to ask, "Where do they go when they can't go home?" Should we just move them in with us?

S: Kathryn, this is a major decision, and since it affects everybody involved, it might be helpful if we discuss certain things people need to consider before they move an elderly person into their own home. One of the first things is whether the elderly person wants to move in with us. This sounds very simple, I know, but some families never bother to even ask the elderly person. They make the decision for them, and start packing them up and moving them. If the elderly person would rather not live with you, then you have lots of options.

K: Gee, you would think most elderly people would rather live with a daughter or son than go to a care facility.

S: Well, believe it or not, that's not always true. Some elderly people think they would be a burden on their family, and so rather than wake up every day, feeling like they are a burden, they would rather live in a care facility. Some individuals realize they would have more opportunities for companionship and to socialize with people their own age if they lived in a facility. Kathryn, sometimes relationships are so strained, due to unresolved issues, that the elderly person just doesn't want to live in the same house with a daughter or son. There may be young children in the home and sometimes children make elderly people nervous; for that reason, the elderly person may not want to live there. Sometimes elderly persons don't even know why they don't want to live with relatives. They just don't want to. And that's okay, too.

K: There are so many things about all this that I've just never thought of. What if they do want to move in with you, and you want them to?

S: In that case, you have to consider a number of things. Is your present home large enough to accommodate another person or two? If your house isn't large enough, then you may have the problems that are inherent in expanding your present home, or maybe you have to find a larger home. I want to mention that renovations and moving are both quite costly. There are subtle expenses that occur, even after you bring another person into your home, such as increased utility and heating bills. Kathryn, some people are on tight budgets, yet they don't think about these things. They go ahead and move the elderly person in. Money gets tight and stress levels go up. Then they start having relationship problems, and sometimes people get into emotional difficulty because they didn't think about certain things ahead of time. Here's another consideration: If you have to move to another neighborhood, maybe because you have to buy a larger house, and you have children, you will need to think about how moving will affect them. They might have to move from their school and from their friends. Also, what effect will moving have on other family members? In some rural areas, people choose to place a mobile home next door to their own home for their parents to live in. Sometimes, they build a smaller house, if they have enough property, but usually that occurs only in very rural areas. Whether you expand your present home, buy a larger house, put a mobile home or smaller house next door to you, there are still many other things you will need to think about.

There are safety issues you must think about.

K: What would be some of those considerations?

S: Can the elderly person be left alone, and if they can, for how long? There are safety issues you must think about. You also need to think about their meals, medications and transportation.

K: Dr. Haymon, it seems like one of the first decisions you have to make is whether your loved one can be left alone. What if they can't stay by themselves?

S: In those situations where it is unsafe for elderly persons to stay at home all day by themselves, you might need to hire someone to come stay with them, just as you would for your children. You would hire a sitter to come in and stay with them while you were at work. In some families, the husband or wife may not work outside the home. Maybe they work at home, so somebody would be there during the day to stay with the elderly person. There may also be the option of taking them to day care during the day and providing in-home care for them at night. However, Kathryn, even in the best of circumstances there are still going to be times and situations when you are going to need help. I recommend that you have a back-up person, maybe a friend or a relative, who would be willing to take care of the elderly person in the event that you become ill or maybe you need to be out of town.

K: What about safety issues at home?

S: When trying to decide whether or not to move your parent(s) in with you, there are many things you normally wouldn't even think about, in terms of safety. However, providing a safe environment for elderly people is quite involved. For example, you will need to ensure there are no rugs they can trip over, and no water on the floors that could cause them to slip. You need to be sure there is no powder on the floors, especially in bathrooms, because that could cause them to slip and fall. You might need to place support handles on the bathtub, raise the level of the toilet seat, or perhaps buy one of those toilet chairs you place over a normal toilet seat. You may need to install special wheelchair ramps, both inside and outside your house. You may need to widen door openings to accommodate walkers and wheelchairs. And, Kathryn, if the individual is disabled or blind, there are even more safety factors that have to be considered. While research does indicate the value of an elderly person having pets with them, some pets present a safety hazard, especially dogs and cats that like to jump and play around people's feet. Besides the safety issues, remember the other problems that I had with pets?

> ...providing a safe environment for elderly people is quite involved.

K: I sure do. I could probably handle the pets, Dr. Haymon, but I would have no idea where to get this equipment — raised toilet seats and things like that. Where did you find them?

S: Well, Kathryn, there are actually a couple of options. Medical supply houses normally carry all this equipment. You might look in the yellow pages under *Medical Supplies*. Also, there are several catalogs that specialize in all sorts of equipment and gadgets for elderly people.

K: Great. You say we need to be concerned about their meals, medication, and transportation. How do we take care of those things?

S: This requires much more consideration than might appear when you first think about it. Many elderly people require special meals, and sometimes they take lots of medications that may have to be taken several times a day. If they are unable to prepare their own meals or eat without supervision, and if they are unable to take their own medications appropriately, then you will need to decide how this is going to be handled. There is also the problem of getting them to and from medical appointments. If they are unable to take public transportation, then somebody will obviously need to drive them. If they are not competent to manage interacting with the doctor, then somebody needs to go with them to talk to the doctor about their condition and get instructions and recommendations. Many elderly people in our country are on dialysis. If this is true for your parent, you will need to decide how she or he is going to be transported to be dialyzed two or three times a week. If they are to be dialyzed at home, how will this be managed? So you see, the decision whether or not to move an elderly person into your home may appear fairly simple at first, but when you really look at it, the decision is very complicated.

> Many elderly people require special meals, and sometimes they take lots of medications that may have to be taken several times a day.

K: I can see that.

S: Before making this decision either way — and I am not trying to persuade anybody one way or the other — but before anybody makes this decision, I would encourage them to talk with every family member this will affect. Talk with the elderly person's medical doctor and with a social worker. I also recommend you find someone who has experienced this and talk with them. It may be that moving an elderly loved one into your home is just not the best option. Although you may want to, and really wish you could, bringing your parents or other elderly loved ones into your home may not be realistic. You may wrestle with a lot of guilt and other emotions about not being able to do so, but it just may not be logistically possible. In most families, both the husband and the wife work, out of necessity. Therefore, it is not feasible for either one of them to quit their job in order to stay home and care for their loved one, even though they wish they could.

K: So if it is not possible for your loved ones to live with you, then how do you decide where to place them?

S: First of all, the type of care facility a person might need depends on her or his required level of care. Once that is determined, there are many options available. Placement options include adult foster homes; these are similar to foster homes for children. There is also congregate community living; these facilities provide apartments or small cluster homes where individuals live independently and take care of most of their own cooking and shopping, yet a nurse or an aide comes by and checks on them every day to ensure they are taking their medications and eating properly, and to take their vital signs. These facilities usually coordinate medical appointments and provide transportation. They may also provide transportation for shopping, attending church, and other personal errands. Most offer ongoing educational talks on nutrition and medications, as well as motivational talks, and some provide church services and spiritual guidance. Sometimes these facilities handle insurance forms and assist with other bill paying. There is often a social-type clubhouse where residents can go to visit, or play cards or shuffle board, or participate in arts and crafts or other social activities. Some even provide driving ranges for golfers. Usually, there are planned social outings to movies, plays, ball games and events of that nature. So as you can see, the services provided by these congregate community homes are endless. It just depends on how much money you want to spend.

There are adult congregate living facilities. This is the type of facility in which I first placed my mother and Carl. These facilities are quite similar to community cluster homes, but instead of living in their own apartment, they actually have a quasi-apartment. They usually have a large bedroom with a walk-in closet, and their own bathroom. The facility prepares all meals and the residents eat together in a large dining room which is normally quite nice, with linen tablecloths and napkins. Residents are often given menus in advance so they may order what they want to eat. For example, at dinner tonight they are given the menus for tomorrow. They would check what they wanted for breakfast, lunch and dinner. These facilities are usually quite nice. However, congregate living facilities require individuals be some-what independent. Normally, residents have to be able to bathe, dress, feed, and toilet themselves. The facility provides nurses on duty 24 hours a day. Medications are given to the residents because they are not normally allowed to have their own medications in their rooms. They also offer planned social activities, both inside and outside the facility. I was really impressed that some of them even provided space for individuals to grow flower and vegetable gardens. The primary goal is to encourage individuals to remain as independent as possible, while still being monitored.

> ...congregate living facilities require individuals be some-what independent. Normally, residents have to be able to bathe, dress, feed, and toilet themselves.

Kathryn, there are also Alzheimer's care facilities which provide care for individuals suffering from different types of dementia. The individual may have a diagnosis of Alzheimer's disease, although that puzzles me. The only way we can truly know if a person has Alzheimer's is to perform an autopsy. Anyway, I think dementia is like a psychiatrist friend once said: "Dementia is dementia — whether you call it Alzheimer's or old-age dementia, or alcohol dementia — and the bottom line is the person experiences thought confusion and disorientation, which may or may not include hostile, aggressive, acting-out behaviors." Since individuals with dementia tend to wander, they live in units that are contained because they are not allowed to go to other areas without an escort. These facilities provide skilled nursing 24 hours a day and medical doctors, including psychiatrists, make rounds. Patients eat their meals under supervision and with assistance, if needed. There are planned activities inside, and sometimes outside the facilities. Often, there are patios or gardens, so residents may safely go outside. There are exercise programs, and beauty and barber shops are often located in the same unit where residents live. Even though they have dementia, residents are encouraged to function at their highest level.

> ...it is so important for the individual's true level of functioning to be accurately assessed before you start looking for a place for her or him to live.

There are long-term care facilities, such as nursing homes. These facilities also provide 24-hour-a- day skilled nursing care. Medical doctors, including psychiatrists, usually make daily rounds. These facilities provide care for individuals ranging anywhere from those who are incontinent and need assistance bathing, dressing, and feeding themselves, to people who are in persistive vegetative states and on feeding tubes.

While many of the services provided by nursing homes are also provided by hospitals, it is less costly to take care of individuals in nursing homes. However, there is limited space in all these facilities, and usually the waiting lists are quite long. So it is not a good idea to postpone making these decisions until the need is urgent.

K: I had no idea there were so many choices.

S: You don't have as much choice as you might think, because every facility has admissions criteria. Remember when I needed a place for my mother? The admissions director said that they had an empty room. I said we would take it. Then I was told that I had to bring Mother in so they could evaluate her and then they would decide whether or not she could live there.

K: Yes.

S: Well, every facility has its own admissions criteria. That is why it is so important for the individual's true level of functioning to be accurately assessed before you start looking for a place for her or him to live. The truth is, if you place them in the wrong facility, you will just wind up moving them. And this is physically and emotionally distressing, not only for the elderly person, but for you as a caregiver, too.

I would like to discuss a couple of other facilities. One is adult day care, which I mentioned earlier. These centers provide day care for individuals who are functioning at a high level. They usually do not accept people with dementia, and some will not even accept those who are incontinent.

There are also rehabilitation centers. They usually provide physical and speech therapy and other types of rehabilitation programs for individuals who have had strokes, surgery, or maybe are recovering from broken hips or other accidents. Usually, rehabilitation centers are short-term and the length of stay is determined by need.

K: Dr. Haymon, what happens if one of your parents is functioning pretty well, but the other one needs a lot of assistance?

S: That's a really good question, Kathryn. There are additional concerns when an elderly couple has to be separated due to their functioning at different levels which require different levels of care. One scenario, which tends to be overwhelming, occurs when one becomes dependent and perhaps needs Medicaid assistance, and the other is still capable of remaining in their home, yet she or he is unable to take care of a spouse. Not only does this separate couples, which causes emotional distress for them, but what you might learn at this point is that for one to receive Medicaid requires disposing of most of their mutual assets. Sometimes this leaves the other spouse with virtually no funds to live on. In other cases, both of them may initially need to live in the same level care facility. Then, weeks or months later, one becomes more disabled than the other, and consequently, has to be moved to a different facility, perhaps one that provides greater care. In my case, I was very surprised to learn that Mother and Carl had to be separated because one was too disabled for a particular care facility and the other wasn't disabled enough. These situations may be extremely emotionally distressing for the elderly persons, as well as for the caregiver.

> I was very surprised to learn that Mother and Carl had to be separated because one was too disabled for a particular care facility and the other wasn't disabled enough.

K: Dr. Haymon, I was surprised to learn that you had to move your stepfather, Carl, 10 times and your mother 6 times in their first year of placement in care facilities. First, I can't even imagine what a drain that was on you and them, and then I wonder why you had to move them so many times.

S: In most cases, as the individual's level of care changes, so does the provider of that care. Since the level of care does not follow a straight line, it is common to experience the need for change in care facilities several times a year. This is common. It might be helpful to visualize a staircase with children playing on it. They start at the top stair, then they hop down a couple of steps, then they jump back up a step, then they hop down three, and they go back up one, and so on and so forth. That is commonly the way it goes.

K: What happened with your parents?

S: Gosh, Kathryn, let's see if I can even remember all that. Well, first of all, remember on that infamous Valentine's Day, Carl had to go to the hospital and my mother had to go to a care facility? Then Carl was dismissed from the hospital to a nursing home facility that provided skilled nursing care 24 hours a day. He was there for less than two weeks when he improved enough that nursing home care was no longer needed. So he was discharged, and we were all very happy about that. However, he then went to a rehabilitation facility.

Well, three days after moving him there, my mother fell and broke her hip. Consequently, she had to go to the hospital. After hip surgery, she was released to a rehabilitation facility. Fortunately, and I do mean, fortunately, I was able to get her in the same rehabilitation center that Carl was already in. I can assure you that due to limited bed space and waiting lists that are usually quite long, that was the exception, rather than the rule. Well, my mother remained in the rehabilitation center for about three weeks, then I was sent a notice that the adult congregate living facility (ACLF) where she had been living was only allowed to hold her room for 30 days. Since she had been hospitalized for several days prior to going to the rehabilitation center, she had been away from her residence facility, the ACLF, for about three weeks when I got the certified letter stating they were only allowed to hold her room for 30 days. I did not learn they were only allowed to hold her bed for 30 days until she had only 7 days remaining. That meant I had to get her functioning at a high enough level that she could go back to the ACLF within a week. So we beefed up all rehabilitation efforts, and I talked her doctor into releasing her to go back to her residence facility. In retrospect, a better decision might have been to have allowed her to remain in the rehabilitation center and just let things take a natural course.

> ...most care facilities don't have many rooms to accommodate couples.

The truth was, rather than going back to the ACLF, my mother really should have been placed in a nursing home. But, Kathryn, I was still in denial. Well, about two weeks after I took Mother back to the ACLF, Carl was also discharged from the rehabilitation center. Although I was able to move him to the same facility, I had to move Mother from the room she shared with another female resident into a room designated for couples so she and Carl could be together. Obtaining a room at the same facility for both of them was, once again, the exception rather than the rule. I felt very, very fortunate that I was able to get Carl in this congregate living facility with my mother.

K: Were you just lucky? The timing was right? What had happened for you to say, "The exception rather than rule?"

S: I guess I was just lucky, because most care facilities don't have many rooms to accommodate couples. These rooms are very limited. Women normally outlive their husbands. Most rooms and bed spaces are for females only, with a few for men only, and even fewer for couples because there just aren't that many couples who live in the same care facility. I was very fortunate to get one of those rooms, because there are so few of them. Anyway, Carl and my mother stayed together at the ACLF, until that incident involving alcohol, when Carl left the facility pushing Mother in her wheelchair, and I was asked to move them.

That's when I moved both of them to a nursing home and, if you will remember, that is when Carl was unable to continue getting alcohol. He was in the nursing home for a couple of weeks, then he had to go to a psychiatric hospital. He stayed there for a couple of weeks. He then came back to the nursing home. He was there for two more weeks, then I had to move him back to the psychiatric center. He developed a bladder infection while he was there, so he then had to go to the hospital, where he underwent minor surgery. He was discharged a few days later, however, I was told at that time that he was no longer appropriate for nursing home care. So I had to move him to an Alzheimer's unit.

Of course, I now know a lot of Carl's acting-out behaviors had to do with alcohol withdrawal. At any rate, there were no beds at any of the local facilities, so I had to move Carl to a facility in another part of the state. This left my mother at one facility, the nursing home, and Carl in another facility, an Alzheimer's unit, which was security-level care. After a couple of months, I was able to move my mother to the Alzheimer's care facility with Carl. They have been there for almost a year. We are just about to celebrate our first year anniversary of nobody moving.

So you can see, in just one year, the number of changes for these two people was incredible. I moved Carl 10 times and my mother 6 times. Sixteen times I was involved in moving these people in one year. I literally thought I would lose my mind. It seemed like a joke. I never knew "who was on first." All of these moves were very distressing for them, not only because they were disturbed about their own moves, but because they were distressed every time the other one moved. And it was extremely distressing for me. It might be helpful to note here that one's required level of care is dynamic — it moves in both directions. That's why I used the analogy of children playing on the stairs, where they hop up one and down two. It seemed to me that several changes came rapidly, then they would level off, followed by another spurt of rapid changes. Every time there is a change, and an elderly person has to be moved, it usually creates anxiety and disorientation for them. Often they become agitated; it is emotionally distressing for them.

> Every time there is a change, and an elderly person has to be moved, it usually creates anxiety and disorientation for them.

Since I had never been through this process, and since I hadn't talked with anyone who had, I could never have anticipated all the steps that would necessarily follow every crisis. I was continually in a state of anxiety myself. I had no idea that being discharged from one facility might mean they could not return to the previous one, nor did I know I would need to find appropriate placement for them at their new level of functioning. I certainly had not conceptualized the notion that there would be many times when they would not be able to stay together because they were functioning at different levels. Kathryn, this is not the worst case scenario, but it is a real life scenario. Honestly, I have had people, when I've done workshops and seminars, come and talk with me afterwards, and my story would pale when I heard theirs. The main point here is, the first time you place your elderly loved one in a care facility, it is probably just that. It is the first of many.

K: I will be honest with you; I am overwhelmed just listening to this. I can't imagine what it must have been like for you.

S: Kathryn, I thought I would lose my mind. Perhaps, if I had not been in denial, or at least if I had gotten some input from others, some of the changes my folks had to endure could have been prevented. Realizing how denial sometimes influences decisions and sometimes paralyzes people from taking any action at all, I strongly encourage people to solicit input from other people. It is very difficult to try to assess the level of functioning for someone you love and care about. You want them to maintain their independence. But remember that every time you move an elderly person she or he may become confused, which may create anxiety and increased feelings of insecurity. So you can see where choosing the wrong living arrangement often results in a number of moves that could probably be avoided if we place them in the proper care facility the first time we place them.

> It is very difficult to try to assess the level of functioning for someone you love and care about.

K: Dr. Haymon, thank you so much for sharing your story and doing all this research on the different care facilities, so we won't have to do it when it becomes our turn. Again, thank you very much.

CHAPTER 6

ASSISTANCE PROGRAMS

K: Dr. Haymon, we have talked about denial, end-of-life medical decisions, advance directives, and living arrangements, and you have told us how expensive elder care is. When you say nursing home care costs as much as $75,000 a year, that's scary. My next question is, who is going to pay? I hear horror stories where elderly people simply do not have enough money to pay, yet they have too many assets to qualify for government programs. What assistance is available? What does it take to qualify?

S: First, let me say any government program I talk about is subject to change. At this time, June, 1996, Congressional leaders are arguing about the federal government turning billions of dollars over to the states and allowing them to figure out how they are going to provide for the elderly. So many of these programs may change, or be eliminated all together.

The last year for which there are any figures available is 1993. Those figures are probably much higher now, but even so, Medicare and Medicaid, the two main government programs, were already paying for about 60% of all nursing home care. That year, those two programs spent over $42 billion on nursing home expenses.

K: How many people are covered by Medicare and Medicaid?

S: According to the 1993 figures, about 1.5 million elderly citizens were receiving help with nursing home bills.

K: Perhaps many folks share my lack of understanding of Medicare. Could you help us understand this federal program?

S: Medicare is our nation's health insurance program. It was initially created in 1966 and is administered by the Social Security Administration. It was created because many older people could not afford to purchase health care insurance. Although Medicare was designed for individuals 65 or older, younger people with certain disabilities, for example, kidney failure, may qualify for Medicare benefits. Medicare provides for basic healthcare, but it does not cover all expenses. Medicare is divided into two parts. Medicare Part A is the hospital insurance part, and Part B is the medical insurance part. Since these are two separate insurance coverages, it might be helpful if we talk about Part A first, and then talk about Part B.

MEDICARE PART A

Medicare Part A, the hospital insurance, is financed by taxes such as the Social Security payroll withholding tax paid by workers and their employers, and the self-employment tax paid by self-employed individuals. These taxes are mandated by the Federal Insurance Contributions Act and are deducted from every paycheck. So when you see a FDIC deduction, which is the Federal Deduction for Insurance Contributions on your pay stub, you will know you are contributing to our national health insurance program. That's why persons 65 or older qualify for *premium free* Medicare Part A, if they are getting Social Security, or Railroad Retirement, because they've already paid it. Even if you're not getting Social Security or Railroad Retirement, but you've worked long enough to qualify for those benefits, you could still be eligible. Also, people who have worked in Medicare-covered government employment could be eligible, if they have worked long enough to be insured for Medicare.

K: Dr. Haymon, no matter how wealthy we are or how much money we make, could we still qualify for premium free Medicare Part A benefits?

S: Yes, because Medicare Part A is funded by FDIC taxes that are automatically deducted from our paychecks, so everybody who has worked enough quarters in Medicare-covered employment would qualify for *premium free* Medicare Part A, which means they don't have to pay monthly premiums. More than 76% of Medicare beneficiaries have annual incomes greater than $25,000 per year. Eighteen percent have incomes between $25,000 and $50,000 per year and another 4% have annual incomes which exceed $50,000 and they are getting Medicare because they have already paid for it.

K: You said nearly every person 65 or older is eligible. How do they apply for *premium free* Medicare Part A?

A: For most people, premium free Medicare Part A starts automatically when they turn 65, if they have retired and are already getting Social Security or Railroad Retirement benefits.

K: What about people who wait until they are 65 to retire?

S: Individuals who are not receiving Social Security or Railroad Retirement when they turn 65 have an initial seven-month enrollment period that begins three months prior to their 65th birthday and ends three months after the month they turn 65. For example, if your birthday is June 15, you would need to contact the Social Security office between March 15 and October 15 to sign up for Medicare Part A and for your Social Security benefits. I suggest people mark their calendars three months in advance of this most important birthday. Individuals who do not enroll during their initial seven-month period would have to wait until the next general enrollment period, which is held January 1 through March 31 of each year.

Disabled widows and widowers between 50 and 65 years of age, who have not applied for disability because they are already receiving some other government assistance, may also apply for Medicare Part A. Individuals who have received Social Security or Railroad Retirement disability benefits for at least 24 months could also be eligible for Part A, as well as those who are receiving kidney dialysis or are kidney transplant patients. I recommend that people contact their local Social Security office and ask.

K: Is the Social Security office the place to begin asking questions about eligibility, enrollment and benefits?

S: Yes. I know this is a lot of information, so I have included summaries of all the programs we're talking about.

K: What about people who do not qualify for premium free Medicare Part A?

S: Individuals 65 or older, who do not qualify for premium free Medicare Part A, may purchase this coverage, but they also must purchase Medicare Part B. You can't buy Part A without also buying Part B. If you buy Part A and Part B, it is no longer premium free coverage.

K: Is that expensive?

S: At present (1996), the monthly premium for Part A is $289 a month for individuals who have fewer than 30 quarters of Medicare-covered employment. The cost is $188 a month for persons with more than 30, but fewer than 40 quarters of covered employment. There is an additional $42.50 a month for Part B, no matter which premium you may have. So the totals would be $331.50, or $230.50, per month, per person, respectively.

The initial seven-month enrollment period for individuals who have to purchase Part A is the same as it is for those who qualify for premium free Medicare Part A. It begins three months prior to her or his 65th birthday and ends three months after the month she or he turns 65. There is a 10% increase in the premium if you do not enroll during the initial enrollment period, but wait until general enrollment. The general enrollment period, you'll recall, is January 1 through March 31 of each year.

K: Is Medicare Part A like any other hospitalization insurance plan?

S: Medicare Part A is very similar to most other hospitalization insurance plans. Part A helps pay for such things as inpatient hospital services and inpatient care in skilled nursing facilities, as well as hospice and some home healthcare services.

K: What's normally covered during inpatient hospital stays?

S: A semi-private room, all meals, medications, lab tests, x-rays, anesthesia, operating and recovery room costs, intensive and coronary care, regular nursing services, medical supplies, rehabilitation services, and preparatory services related to kidney transplant surgery.

K: Will Part A pay for everything, no matter how long the person is in the hospital?

S: No. Part A helps pay for up to 90 days of medically necessary care in Medicare-participating hospitals during each benefit period. Let me stop here and explain what a benefit period is. A benefit period starts the day the individual is admitted to a hospital or skilled nursing facility, and ends when she or he has been out of the hospital or skilled nursing facility for 60 consecutive days, counting the day of discharge. There is no limit to the number of benefit periods an individual may have during any given calendar year.

In-patient Hospital Deductibles

Now let me talk about the deductibles. There is a deductible for every benefit period. At present (1996), that deductible is $736. For example, if you had three admissions to a hospital in any given year, and those were during three separate benefit periods, that would be over $2,000 you would have to pay out-of-pocket. Once you've paid the deductible, for that benefit period, Part A would pay for all covered medical services during the first 60 days of inpatient hospital care, then Part A would pay for all covered medical services except for $184 a day for days 61 through 90. If you remain hospitalized after 90 days, you have 60 reserve days which you may use for days 91 through 150. Part A would pay for everything except for $368 a day for those additional 60 days. You may use the 60 reserve benefit days at your discretion, however, you only have 60 reserve benefit days to use within your lifetime. Those reserve days are not renewable. Even if you remain in the hospital beyond 90 days, you might not want to use your reserve days. Perhaps you have some other insurance coverage that would pay. You must notify the hospital, in writing, ahead of time, that you do not plan to use your reserve days. If you elect to use your reserve days, you would be responsible for all charges beyond 150 days, because Medicare Part A would pay nothing after that.

Skilled Nursing Care

If you were admitted to a skilled care facility, after you have had a hospital stay of at least three days, Medicare Part A would pay 100% of the covered charges for the first 20 days, then Part A would pay all but $92 a day for an additional 80 days. Beyond those 100 days, Medicare Part A pays nothing for skilled nursing care. If you were residing in a care facility prior to your hospital stay, there could be a problem with maintaining your room or bed space at your residence facility. Even though Medicare Part A allows for 100 days of skilled care, most residence facilities will only hold your room or bed space for a predetermined number of days. For example, when my mother's hip was broken and she went from the congregate living facility to the hospital, then to a rehabilitative skilled care facility, Medicare helped pay for 100 days, as long as she was improving. But here's the irony: It wasn't practical for her to stay the entire 100 days, even though Medicare would have helped pay for it, because the congregate living facility where she lived would only hold her bed for 30 days. My mom actually had 100 days of coverage, which she needed in order to fully recover, but her bed would only be held for 30 days from the time she first left the congregate living facility.

It gets to be a real Catch-22 for elderly who live in care facilities and have to worry about what's covered and what happens to their room or bed space at their residence facility. If they stay in the hospital or rehabilitative center the full length of time, they may risk losing their bed and going to the end of the waiting line for another one. There are lots of things you have to pay close attention to. I also need to mention that when a person is in a rehabilitative center, once her or his progress stops, and the physician sees no improvement in ability to function, Medicare stops paying at that point.

Other Covered Services

Medicare Part A would pay 100% of approved charges for part-time or intermittent skilled home care, and 80% of durable medical equipment and supplies for an unlimited time, as long as you meet Medicare requirements. Medicare Part A helps pay for hospice care, and for blood furnished by a hospital or skilled nursing facility. You have to pay for, or replace, the first three pints of blood per calendar year, but starting with the fourth pint, Medicare would pay for as much blood as deemed medically necessary. Medicare Part A would also help pay for psychiatric hospital care and for inpatient services provided by Medicare-participating Christian Science sanatoriums.

K: There seem to be a lot of things that need to be coordinated when a person is discharged from the hospital. If you are unable to handle these things, is there a service that would take care of this for you?

S: When an individual is discharged from the hospital, usually a social worker, who may actually be employed by the hospital, will make arrangements for the person's specific needs. For example, the social worker would arrange for transportation and any recuperation assistance the patient might need, or arrangements for long-term care, or perhaps homemaking assistance.

Part-time/Intermittent Skilled Home-Care

K: You said Medicare Part A would help pay for part-time or intermittent home health visits for people who are confined in their homes. What sort of home health care would be paid for?

S: That's true, Part A would pay as long as the home healthcare agency is approved by Medicare, and as long as the physician writes an order stating that the person needs home healthcare. In that case, Medicare Part A normally covers services which include medical supplies and equipment, speech, physical and occupational therapy, medical social services, and part-time skilled nursing care. Normally, there is no limit to the number of covered visits, however, Medicare Part A does not pay for custodial care, such as help with bathing, dressing, or going to the bathroom, if that's the only type of care a person needs.

K: How does skilled nursing care differ from non-skilled nursing care?

S: In order to qualify for skilled nursing care, the patient must have a diagnosis from a medical doctor for treatment that requires a registered nurse or other licensed personnel. Non-skilled nursing care does not require a registered nurse or licensed personnel. For example, an IV would require skilled care, but a catheter probably would not.

Hospice

K: You also said that Medicare Part A would pay for hospice. I understand that's a special kind of care primarily for terminally-ill patients. What kind of hospice services would Part A pay for?

S: Medicare Part A would pay for hospice care, as long as the care is provided by a Medicare-certified hospice program. Normally, Medicare Part A will cover such expenses as doctors' and nurses' services, drugs for the relief of pain, medical supplies and appliances, speech therapy, physical therapy, medical social services, counseling, home health aide services, some homemaker services, and almost all of the cost of respite care, which is short-term, inpatient care intended to give temporary relief to individuals who regularly assist with home care. Medicare Part A pays for almost everything regarding hospice care. There may be a co-payment of up to $5 for each prescription medication and about $5 per day for inpatient respite care. Medicare Part A provides for 4 benefit periods of hospice care; two 90-day periods, one 30-day period, and a 4th period which is unlimited. So that is 210 days of hospice care normally covered by Medicare Part A. However, when those 210 days run out, if the patient still needs hospice care, then Medicare must continue paying. That's when the 4th, unlimited, benefit period comes in.

K: That seems a little confusing. In other words, you are saying there are rules, and yet sometimes those rules may be broken.

S: Well, let me see if I can explain it this way. Cancer is a little different than a lot of illnesses. The person may be very, very ill for two or three months and require hospice care. Then the cancer might go into remission and the person may do really well, sometimes even for years. Then the symptoms return and the person needs hospice care again. Medicare Part A would then resume paying for hospice. So you can see how a person might not use all 210 days at one time. The bottom line is, if hospice is involved in the person's care, when the 210 days run out Medicare Part A must continue paying until the person dies or elects conventional care. Even though you might have chosen hospice for treatment of a terminal illness, you still have the option of using Medicare Part A's standard benefits for treatment of a condition other than the terminal illness. In that case, you would have to pay the deductibles and co-payments.

Medicare Part A Claims

K: **Does Medicare pay the hospital or home healthcare agency directly, or does the person have to pay first, then get reimbursed?**

S: Federal law requires that all providers of medical services file Medicare claims for patients, even if the provider is not a Medicare participant. Therefore, the provider of medical services is always paid directly by Medicare Part A. The provider is paid the percentage allowed by Medicare. Medical providers have 24 months from the date of the service to submit claims to Part A. Individuals may be required to pay their deductibles and co-insurance amounts, as well as any non-covered services, at the time they receive the services, or they might be billed for those expenses later. This is where it might be helpful to have a supplemental insurance policy.

K: **Is there a maximum amount Medicare Part A will pay? Is there a cap?**

S: It isn't really a cap in terms of dollar amount. The maximum amount Medicare Part A will pay depends on what day in the benefit period you are being charged for and whether you are in a hospital or skilled care facility. As I mentioned earlier, if you are in a hospital, Medicare Part A will pay for everything except the $736 deductible during the first 60 days of each benefit period, however, if you are in the hospital between 60 and 90 days, Medicare Part A would pay for everything except $184 a day. If you are in a skilled care facility, 100% of the approved amount is covered for the first 20 days.

K: **Thank you Dr. Haymon, I believe I am beginning to understand Medicare Part A.**

SUMMARY

ASSISTANCE PROGRAMS AND BENEFITS

Information regarding these programs, addresses,
and phone numbers is subject to change.

MEDICARE

Federal Insurance Program

- Developed in 1966 by the Health Care Financing Administration of The U. S. Department of Health and Human Services
- Social Security offices take applications and provide assistance
- For individuals 65 and older and people with certain disabilities

---

MEDICARE PART A: HOSPITAL INSURANCE (current for 1996)

Eligibility Requirements for Premium Free Medicare Part A:

65 or older

- Persons receiving Social Security (SS) or Railroad Retirement (RR) are automatically enrolled
- Individuals who have not filed for Social Security or Railroad Retirement are eligible to enroll
- Medicare-covered government employees

Under 65

- Individuals disabled for more than 24 months and drawing disability are automatically enrolled
- Government employees who have been disabled more than 29 months
- Individuals who are on continuous dialysis, or who have had a kidney transplant

Enrollment Period:

- Initial seven-month period begins three months before 65th birthday and continues three months after the birth month

General Enrollment Period – January 1 - March 31 of each year

- Benefits begin the following July

Eligibility Requirements to Purchase Medicare Part A:

- Individuals 65 or older, who do not have enough work quarters to qualify for premium free
- Individuals who are disabled, yet do not qualify for premium free because they are working

Enrollment Period:

- Initial seven-month enrollment period begins three months before 65th birthday and continues for three months after the birth month

General Enrollment Period – January 1 - March 31 of each year

- Benefits begin the following July after general enrollment
- May be charged an additional 10% surcharge in monthly premiums, unless covered by a group health plan for the months the person could have been enrolled, but was not
- Individuals covered by an HMO may enroll any time and up to eight months after coverage ends, and the premium surcharge may be waived

Benefit Period:
- Begins first day of inpatient care
- Ends when individual has been out of hospital or skilled care facility for 60 consecutive days, including day of discharge
- No limit to number of benefit periods within calendar year

Hospital Inpatient:

Deductibles

$736 each benefit period

Co-Insurance — Your share of Costs

Days 01- 60 = Deductible of $736

Days 61- 90 = $184 per day

Days 91-150 = $368 per day (60 Reserve Days)

Days 151+   = You pay for all expenses

Reserve Days
- 60 in lifetime
- All covered services, except $368 per day

Covered Services:
- Semi-private room
- Meals
- Nursing care
- Special Care Units (intensive/coronary)
- Drugs
- Blood transfusions
- Lab tests included in hospital bill
- X-Rays/radiology services
- Medical supplies (casts, surgical dressings, splints, etc.)
- Use of appliances (wheelchairs, walkers, etc.)
- Operating/recovery room
- Rehabilitation services (physical/occupational/speech therapy)

Some Services NOT Covered:
- Personal comfort items (telephone/television)
- Private duty nurse
- Private room, unless determined medically necessary

Skilled Nursing Facility (Must meet all five criteria)
- Inpatient stay three days or longer, not counting day of discharge
- Require daily skilled nursing care
- Admitted within 30 days of hospital discharge
- Care is for condition treated in hospital
- Medical professional certifies patient needed and received skilled care

Benefits:

Days 1 - 20   = 100% of covered amount

Days 21-100 = All but $92 per day

Days 101+   = You pay for all charges

Covered Services:
- Semi-private room
- Meals
- Nursing care
- Physical/occupational/speech therapy
- Drugs
- Blood transfusions
- Medical supplies (splints, casts, etc.)
- Use of appliances (wheelchairs, walkers, etc.)

Some Services NOT Covered:
- Personal comfort items (television, telephones)
- Private duty nurses
- Private room, unless determined medically necessary
- Services not provided by facility, but included in bill
- Part A does not pay doctor services — Part B does

Home Health Services (Must meet all four criteria)

- Confined to home
- Physician determines need and sets up care plan
- Needed care includes: intermittent skilled nursing, or physical or speech therapy
- Agency is Medicare-participant

Covered Services
- Number of days are unlimited — 100% approved charges
- Durable, medical equipment — 80% of approved charges
- Part-time/intermittent skilled nursing care
- Home health aide services
- Physical/speech/occupational therapy
- Medical social services
- Medical supplies

Some Services NOT Covered:
- 24-hour-a-day nursing
- Drugs/biologicals
- Meals delivered
- Homemaker services
- Blood transfusions

Psychiatric Hospital

- 190 days inpatient care within a lifetime
- Psychiatric care in general hospitals is usually not subject to 190 day-limit

Christian Science Sanatorium

- Helps pay for inpatient hospital/skilled nursing facility (operated, listed and certified by The First Church of Christ, Scientist, Boston, Massachusetts)

Hospice: Pain Relief, Symptom Management, Support Services
(Must meet all three criteria)

- Doctor certifies patient is terminally ill
- Patient chooses hospice care, instead of standard Medicare-approved treatment
- Medicare-participating hospice program

Benefits:

- 210 days covered, as long as doctor certifies need
- All but $5 for each prescription
- All but $5 per day for approved inpatient respite care

Covered Services

- Regular Medicare Part A may help pay for treatments not related to terminal illness
- Doctors and nurses
- Drugs
- Physical/occupational/speech therapy
- Home health aide and homemaker services
- Medical social services
- Medical supplies and appliances
- Short-term inpatient care
- Counseling
- Blood
 ~ furnished during covered stay
 ~ all but first three pints per calendar year
 ~ unlimited, if medically necessary

Some Services NOT Covered:

- Treatments other than for pain relief and symptom management

BRIEF SUMMARY

MEDICARE PART A: Hospital Insurance

Deductible:

  $736 each benefit period

Benefits:

  Hospital

Days 01- 60	= All covered expenses are paid after deductible ($736) is met
Days 61- 90	= All but $184 Per Day
Days 91- 150	= All but $368 Per Day (60 Reserve Days)

Skilled Nursing

Days 1 - 20	= 100% covered
Days 21-100	= All but $92 per day
Days 101+	= Pays nothing

Medical Supplies And Equipment

  80% of approved charges

Medicare Part B, see pages 82-92.

DRGs

K: Let's move on to something called "Diagnosis-Related Group Decisions." I have heard this referred to as DRGs. What are DRGs?

S: DRGs, Diagnosis-Related Group Decisions, are classifications of specific conditions. Medicare Part A will pay a flat fee for each patient hospitalized under those classifications. Allow me to use the example, once again, of when my mother fell and broke her hip. The amount Medicare Part a will pay for broken hips (and other specific conditions), is based on a DRG decision. The DRG decision determines the flat amount Medicare Part A will pay for all broken hips. When my mother broke her hip and was admitted to the hospital, the physician knew exactly how much Medicare would pay for a broken hip. When that dollar amount has been used, it is in the hospital's best interest, financially, to get you out of there, whether your hip is healed or not. Hospitals are driven by money. They can't afford to have you hanging around for two or three days longer than they're being reimbursed for. When that amount is used, you're going somewhere else. You're either going to a rehabilitative center, or you're going home, or you may be going to a homeless shelter, but when that pre-determined amount is used, you will be discharged from the hospital.

K: The doctor or hospital may not really have a choice; that's what I'm hearing.

S: Providers really don't have a choice. They have to abide by DRG decisions.

K: What if you disagree with the DRG decision?

S: You do have the right to appeal any DRG decision. When a member of a hospital staff tells you it's the last day Medicare Part A will pay for, they must give you notice in writing. Then, if you call the Professional Review Organization by noon the day after you get this notice, you will not be liable for any covered hospital charges until the Professional Review Organization informs you in writing of their decision. The Professional Review Organization may be contacted by calling Medicare Customer Services at 1-800-772-1213.

K: If the DRG decision directs that a broken hip, or other condition, is only allowed a certain number of days, wouldn't you normally have more advanced notice than the day the hospital is releasing you? Wouldn't you know the DRG decision states that you can only be there for 30 days to fix your hip?

S: I wouldn't say you normally know that, no. If I knew then, what I know now, every time my mother or stepfather was admitted for any reason I would have asked up front: What is the diagnosis? Is this based on a DRG decision? If it is, how much will Medicare Part A pay, and how does that translate in terms of the number of days Medicare Part A will pay for? You see, it gets real simple. What's the diagnosis? Is it based on a classification for DRG decision? How much will they pay? How long can she stay? Asking all of that ahead of time gives you some idea about when your loved one will be released, so you can make arrangements.

K: Thank you for helping us to better understand Diagnosis-Related Group Decisions.

Medicare Part A and Nursing Homes

K: Are the waiting lists for beds in nursing homes longer for individuals who are dependent on Medicare Part A or Medicaid, compared to private pay patients?

S: Surprisingly enough, Medicare Part A patients usually get preferential treatment, because Medicare Part A pays more than private pay individuals and it pays a lot more than Medicaid pays. As a matter of fact, many facilities prefer patients who have not used their 100 skilled nursing days. On the average, individuals use about 57 of their 100 days. If they have a lot of days remaining, they get preferential treatment as far as bed space in nursing homes is concerned. In some nursing homes, there are over 100 patients on the waiting lists at any given time, and it could be as long as four or five years before someone on Medicaid could even get a bed. There are many facilities that report their waiting lists are six to nine months for individuals who do not come directly from a hospital. Other facilities are quick to acknowledge that they prefer to take individuals from Medicare Part A and continue providing care for them through Medicaid, after Medicare Part A benefits have expired. Although it is considered a last resort for coverage, Medicaid finances the largest portion of nursing home bills. Medicaid paid some $38 billion dollars in nursing home charges in 1993, but many nursing homes that acknowledge they couldn't operate without Medicaid funds still give Medicaid patients lowest priority. They put them on waiting lists for months, even years.

We'll talk about Medicaid in a minute, but right now it might be helpful to talk about the process of finding a nursing home. You could start by contacting your Area Agency on Aging. Sometimes they will even do a free assessment to help you determine what services your elderly loved one needs. Even if they don't provide that service, they will refer you to organizations that will do evaluations. However, when you call any organization, ask, up front, what the charges are. Some companies actually charge high prices for information that many state agencies provide free.

Consumer Reports compiled a comprehensive listing of nursing home chains and reported these from best to worst in the August, 1995 issue. This was the first report of its kind. Those people looking for a nursing home might want to go to a library and retrieve the article, "Nursing Homes, When a Loved One Needs Care," or you could call *Consumer Reports* at 1-800-234-1645 or 1-941-378-2740, and ask for a reprint of that article.

K: What are your recommendations for ways to pay for nursing home care for our loved ones?

S: Don't depend on Medicare Part A alone. It only pays for nursing home care if it's required after a hospital stay, and it will pay for no more than 100 days of nursing home care during any benefit period. One hundred days is a very brief period for an elderly person to be in a nursing home. I recommend that individuals purchase long-term care insurance. Many of those policies will pay a daily rate somewhere between $50 and $200, and that can help defray some of the cost when your loved one has to be in a nursing home. The provisions of these policies vary from short periods of supplemental coverage, perhaps for one year, to an indefinite period of time extending until the person dies. Of course, premiums vary accordingly. If you're purchasing a long-term care policy several years before you expect to need it, then you also need to ensure it has an inflation rider on it. Many of these riders increase the value of the coverage about five per cent a year.

K: Dr. Haymon, through all of this have you come up with recommendations for individuals who are looking for someone to care for their parents in their own home?

S: Should you need to hire someone to come into your parents' home, be sure they are bonded, or the company they work for has them bonded. That may offer you some recourse, if theft or something else occurs. Also, be sure the company carries workers' compensation insurance on the workers, so that if they are injured while working on your property, they are at least covered by workers' compensation. It's common for workers to get back injuries when they are caring for elderly people. Sometimes, the caregiver has to pull the elderly person up to help her or him get out of bed, or the elderly person may be about to fall and the caregiver reaches to catch her or him. The likelihood of someone getting injured is pretty high when dealing with elderly people.

K: If you bring in an adult sitter, will your home insurance cover you against that liability, if they don't have workers' compensation?

S: That's a good question. I recommend that you contact your homeowner's insurance company and ask whether persons you hire to come to your parents' home, or to your home, are covered if they are injured. You might need to specify *injured,* because an *accident* might be covered, whereas an *injury* might not be. For example, a worker might fall down the stairs and break her or his leg; that might be covered. If she or he claimed a back injury from helping the elderly person out of bed, that might not be covered by homeowner's insurance. Also, specify that you have actually *hired* the person, because sometimes insurance policies will cover people who are *visiting* in your home and have an accident or become injured, but won't cover people who are actually *working* in your home.

Another recommendation I have is that when you contact a home healthcare provider, you need to specify *exactly* what you want the caregiver to do. Please don't assume they will come in and merely use common sense. I don't mean this in any derogatory manner, but you need to be very, very specific from the start. I recommend you make a list. Write down everything you want the caregiver to do, or to help your parent do. You may have to be as specific as to state that you want the caregiver to help your loved one up to walk around the room three times a day for exercise, or that the caregiver will have to get your parent up and actually help her or him to the bathroom. If you don't specify that, the caregiver might just put a bed pan underneath them and never get them up. Whatever services you think your parents are going to need, write them down, make a list. When you are looking for a company to provide service for your parents, state *exactly* what you want them to do, then have some agent of that company actually sign your list. That way, they can't come back later, when you're complaining that your mother hasn't gotten out of bed for three days, or her hair hasn't been shampooed in a week, and say they didn't know you wanted them to do that. Do you see where I am going with this?

K: Yes, I do.

S: Don't let them intimidate you. Remember, you're the one purchasing service from them. You have every right to know what you are paying for. You also have every right to expect, when you hire someone to come in and take care of your parents, that they are going to do exactly that, they are going to take care of them.

Here is another thing. You will also need to be sure the company has backup personnel. It might surprise you to know that many companies have no backup personnel. In that case, you could get a phone call at 7:30 one morning, telling you the person assigned to your folks cannot be there that day. At that point, it becomes your problem. So ask the company how they handle it if the assigned caregiver is unable to work.

Another important factor is to ensure that the person assigned to your parents is compatible with them. Being old and infirm, maybe even bedridden, is stressful enough without having to spend hour after hour with somebody you really don't like, or that you're just not compatible with. You will want to make some surprise visits to be sure the person is doing what you hired her or him to do, and to observe the person's interactions with your parents. Talk to your mom and dad and ask if they like this person. Sometimes, they won't like anybody that you bring in, but you'll know when that's the case. You'll know when they just don't want anybody in their house, but you can make a better assessment when you observe your parent(s) with the caregiver.

You will also need to check your loved one for bedsores. I don't know how to stress this strongly enough. Bedsores are a common problem and can be extremely painful. Far too often, the elderly person is in so much pain already, she or he may not even notice when there is additional pain. Many elderly people never complain about anything. So even if they don't want to roll over, even if they complain about having to get up, even if it's embarrassing for you, you are going to have to put your embarrassment on the shelf, roll them over, and see if they have bedsores. If there are bedsores, seek medical treatment and, by all means, talk with the caregiver and be very clear about how unacceptable this is.

MEDICARE PART B: MEDICAL

K: Dr. Haymon, what is Medicare Part B and how does it differ from Part A?

S: It might be helpful if I recap Part A before we move on to Part B. Medicare Part A is our national hospitalization insurance program to which nearly everyone is entitled, because they have paid income taxes. It doesn't matter how much money you make, if you qualify, you are entitled to *premium free* Medicare Part A. You automatically qualify for Medicare Part A at age 65 if you are already getting Social Security or Railroad Retirement.

Now let's talk about Part B. Medicare Part B is optional medical insurance. Part B is financed, in part, by monthly premiums that are paid by individuals who elect to enroll in this program. However, I am told, about 75% of Medicare Part B is funded by the federal government. Normally, anyone 65 or older may enroll in Medicare Part B by paying a monthly premium which at present (1996), is $42.50 per month. There is also an annual deductible, which is presently $100. The deductible, monthly premiums, and co-payments, which are the individual's share of costs for Part B, are separate and distinct from those required by Medicare Part A. These are two separate insurance policies: Part A covers hospitalization; Part B, covers medical services.

After the $100 deductible is met, Medicare Part B pays 80% of the amount allowed by Medicare for all approved charges. The individual is responsible for paying the remaining 20%, as well as any unapproved charges. However, should you receive outpatient services at a hospital, your portion of the bill could be 20% of whatever the hospital charges, rather than 20% of the Medicare approved amount. For outpatient mental health services, your part would be 50% of the amount approved by Medicare. In addition, you are responsible for all charges for services you receive that are not Medicare-approved.

K: Let me ask you this: Would I enroll in Part B at the same time I become eligible for Part A?

S: Yes.

K: Can anyone buy it, even if they have a pre-existing medical condition? Is there any reason why they couldn't buy Part B during that period.

S: You have to be enrolled in premium free Part A or purchase Part A at the same time you purchase Part B. If you do not qualify for premium free Part A, you may purchase only Medicare Part A, if that is all you want and you qualify for it, but you can't purchase Part B without getting Part A.

K: But there is no pre-existing condition limitation?

S: No. Individuals who do not sign up during their seven-month initial enrollment period, but then change their minds and want to enroll later, may enroll during a general enrollment period which runs from January 1 through March 31 of every year. However, their medical coverage will not actually start until the following July.

K: Why is that?

S: Well, we are already talking about elderly people. Many of them are frail and have medical problems. Let's say you did not enroll in Medicare Part B at age 65. Now you're 80 and just found out you have some serious medical disorder. You decide to enroll because you need coverage immediately. It would be too costly to allow people to do that. When you purchase private medical insurance, it is common for there to be a waiting period of 30, 60, or 90 days before coverage begins, even for those of us who are healthy.

Here is another thing. For every 12-month period a person could have been enrolled in Medicare Part B, but wasn't, their monthly premium will go up 10%. So let's say you could have enrolled at 65 and now you're 75. That's 10% per year, times 10 years, so your premium would actually be 100% more. Instead of $42.50 per month it would be $85 per month.

K: Is there any reason you wouldn't enroll in Medicare Part B during the initial seven-month period around your 65th birthday?

S: The primary reason people don't buy Part B is because they are already covered under an insurance program that would pay for these services. And sometimes, Kathryn, people just don't have the money. They are not covered by another insurance policy, yet as difficult as it may be for many of us to believe, another $42.50 a month is more than some people can come up with.

K: I guess what I'm asking is, if you had the money, and you had private insurance, would you still buy Medicare Part B?

S: That's a very good question, because every insurance policy is different. You have to look at what you have, look at what will be paid, look at how much it costs you, then decide which one is better for you.

K: Is Part B basically for people who are retiring from a job and would no longer have the insurance coverage that was previously provided by their company?

S: Yes, and although some companies continue to provide insurance after the person retires, individuals would need to compare that coverage and the amount of those monthly premiums with the coverages and monthly premiums for Medicare Part B.

K: So you wouldn't necessarily have private insurance and Part B together?

S: Not necessarily. I can tell you, though, for $42.50 per month, with the things that Medicare Part B covers, it's a bargain. Having gone through it with my own mother and stepfather, I would highly recommend that people who are eligible for Part B, and not totally covered by some other insurance program, come up with $42.50 per month and purchase it.

K: Does Part B pay the doctor and other providers directly, like Part A does?

S: Yes, however, the amount of co-insurance you would be responsible for would depend on whether the doctor or medical supplier accepts *assignment*. You always need to ask the doctors or medical suppliers if they accept assignment. In cases where assignment is accepted, you would sign the Medicare Part B form. After the provider has filed the claim, Medicare Part B would reimburse them directly for 80% of all approved charges. You would be responsible for 20%. The medical provider could ask you to pay the 20% co-payment immediately, but could not charge you more than that.

In *unassigned* cases, those cases in which doctors or medical suppliers do not accept assignment, by federal law, they are allowed to charge you an additional 15%, but not more than that, over the Medicare-approved amount. This means you would actually be responsible for 35% of the charges. They could also ask you to pay the full amount immediately, then after the claim has been filed and approved, Medicare would pay the 80% of the approved amount directly to you. It may be to your advantage to use doctors and medical suppliers who accept assignment, because it could save you as much as 15% of the bill. In addition, doctors who do not accept assignment for elective surgeries are required, by law, to provide you with a written estimate of your costs prior to the surgery, if the amount exceeds $500. If you are not given a written estimate, you are entitled to a refund of any amount you paid over the amount approved by Medicare.

K: Will most medical offices accept assignment?

S: Yes, but they are not legally obligated to.

K: Sounds to me like it would be a good idea, before you get treatment, to know what the provider accepts, as far as Medicare is concerned. Is that true?

S: That is true. You want to be sure they are participants with Medicare. You also want to be sure they're willing to accept assignment, so that you would not be responsible for more than 20% of the amount approved by Medicare Part B.

Medicare Part B Claims

K: Are there time limits for submitting Medicare Part B claims?

S: Yes. All claims must be received by the Medicare Part B office no later than 15 months after the date of the service. Any claim received later than 15 months from the date of the service must be accompanied by an explanation as to why the claim is being filed late. Such a claim would then be submitted to the Part B review board for determination as to whether it would be paid. I am told that the exception to this rule is for outpatient hospital services. Although these services are covered by Part B, they are processed by Part A, and therefore you would have 24 months from the date of service to have your claim in. Doctors and medical service providers who submit claims later than 12 months after the date of the service are charged a 10% penalty, but that would not affect you.

K: What specific procedures or services are covered by Part B?

S: Medicare Part B is the medical coverage. Services rendered by a medical doctor and determined to be medically necessary are covered, regardless of where you receive them—in the doctor's office, medical clinic, nursing home, hospital, or in your own home. Services of some specially qualified practitioners may be covered, although they may not be medical doctors.

Medicare Part B usually covers such medical services as outpatient hospital services; ambulance transportation; blood, after the first three pints per calendar year; flu, pneumonia and hepatitis B immunizations; artificial limbs and eyes; breast prostheses following a mastectomy; anesthesia, x-rays and laboratory tests; radiology and pathology services; physical, occupational, and speech therapy; arm, leg, neck and back braces; outpatient mental health services; certain home-healthcare services; durable medical equipment prescribed by a medical doctor, such as walkers, wheelchairs, hospital beds and oxygen equipment; pap smears for the detection of cervical cancer; mammograms to screen for breast cancer; and some prostate tests. In addition, kidney dialysis and kidney transplants are covered and, under certain conditions, liver and heart transplants received in Medicare-approved facilities would be covered. Surgical dressings, splints, casts, ostomy bags and other medical supplies are also covered. Part B usually pays for 50% of approved, outpatient mental health services, as I said earlier.

As you can see, it is important for people to have either Medicare Part B, or some other insurance policy, which will cover outpatient services not covered by Part A— the hospitalization part of Medicare. Supplemental insurance may also be helpful in covering certain outpatient services that are not covered by Medicare Part B, such as custodial care. Remember, those were services such as bathing, dressing, toileting, and things that could be handled by non-skilled medical personnel. Those are not covered by Part A or Part B.

K: Will any insurance cover that?

S: Yes, but here again, you would need to check each policy to see what it will and will not pay for. There are other services that Medicare Part B will not pay for. Care that you receive outside of the United States is not covered. Neither are routine physical exams or tests related to those exams, nor routine dental care, nor dentures. Part B does not pay for routine foot care, medical tests in reference to eyes or hearing, eyeglasses, hearing aids, acupuncture, or any routine chiropractic services. Medicare Part B usually does not pay for Christian Science practitioners, nor does it pay for any personal comfort items like television, or telephone. Medicare Part B doesn't cover full-time, at home, nursing care. It would pay for part-time, skilled nursing care. That means Part B would pay for the very minimum a nurse would need to provide. If a nurse had to go to your private home and give you an injection, or check an IV, Medicare Part B would pay for just the minimum. Part B will not pay if you need someone at home, full-time. It does not pay for injections you could give to yourself. For example, it's not uncommon for people to give themselves allergy or insulin injections. If the person is capable of doing that, Medicare Part B is not going to pay for someone to come out and do it for her or him. It doesn't pay for meals to be delivered to the home, or for most cosmetic surgery. Medicare Part B is not going to pay for any services that are not reasonable and necessary. I have included a summary of Part B for an easy reference.

Kathryn, I want to take just a moment to talk about a frame of mind that seems to be common for elderly people. Most of these people worked hard their entire lives and are of the opinion or belief that they never want a *handout.* They never want to be on any sort of government program. But you know, Kathryn, many people who are 75, 85 or 90 years old had been working for years before there was Social Security. The Social Security Administration was not formed until 1935, and even then, many jobs were exempt from paying Social Security for employees.

So if your elderly loved one is of this mind set, I recommend that you sit down with her or him and talk about Medicare and other programs. Many elderly people don't realize they have already paid FDIC taxes, or even what those taxes are. It's not a handout, it's something they deserve to get back. They worked to help build this country. Now they need psychological permission to accept back part of what they have already given.

MEDICARE PART B: MEDICAL INSURANCE

Eligibility Requirements
• Individuals must qualify for premium free Medicare Part A or purchase Medicare Part A

Enrollment Period
• Initial seven-month period begins three months before 65th birthday and continues three months beyond the birth month
• Enrollment after 65th birthday could cause a delay in coverage
• If not enrolled during initial seven-month period, cannot enroll until the general enrollment

General Enrollment
• January 1 - March 31 of each year
• Benefits begin the following July
• Premium surcharge for late enrollment (unless covered by other healthcare plan)
  ~ monthly premiums increase 10% for each 12 months the person could have been enrolled, but was not
• Federal law requires individual state Medicaid to pay Medicare costs for low income people

Providers
• Must abide by Medicare laws
• Must file claims for patients, even if they do not accept assignment
• Have 15 months from date of service to file claims

Deductibles:
• $100 each calendar year
• First three pints of blood received each calendar year must be paid for or replaced unless this has been met under Part A
• Starting with the fourth pint of blood, Part B pays 80% of approved charges
• Immunizations are exempt from the deductible

Monthly Premiums:
• $42.50, but may change the first of each year

Co-Insurance
• 20% of approved amount, if on assignment
• If not on assignment, patient pays 20% co-insurance, plus up to 15% more than approved amount, and for all unapproved services

Covered Services:
• Unlimited medical services deemed necessary and provided by Medicare-participating medical doctors or other approved professionals
• Inpatient/outpatient medical services and supplies
• Inpatient/outpatient surgical services and supplies
• Physical and speech therapy
• Diagnostic tests
• Mammograms to screen for breast cancer
• Pap smears for the detection of cervical cancer

- Some tests for prostate cancer
- Flu, pneumonia and Hepatitis B immunizations
- Ambulance services to/from closest hospital or skilled nursing facility when transportation in other vehicles would endanger health
- Air ambulance, only in urgent emergencies, or when land ambulance would endanger health
- Durable medical equipment
  - ~ must be prescribed by medical doctor
  - ~ must be able to withstand repeated use
  - ~ may be purchased or rented
  - ~ wheelchairs
  - ~ lift mechanism for seat-lift chairs
  - ~ power operated vehicles
  - ~ equipment for care of pressure sores (bedsores)
  - ~ orthotics
  - ~ other medically necessary equipment for in-home use
  - ~ back, neck, and leg braces
  - ~ hospital beds
  - ~ oxygen equipment prescribed for home use
- Prosthetics
  - ~ to replace internal organs
  - ~ artificial limbs and eyes
  - ~ corrective lenses after cataract surgery
  - ~ ostomy bags
  - ~ breast prostheses (including surgical brassiere after mastectomy)
- Therapeutic shoes
  - ~ diabetic foot disease — one pair per calendar year
  - ~ inserts or modifications
  - ~ fittings
- Second opinions regarding surgery
- Third surgical opinions, if first two contradict
- Ambulatory surgical services (hospital stay not required)
- Medical doctors
  - ~ medical and surgical services
  - ~ anaesthesia
  - ~ diagnostic tests/procedures as part of treatment
  - ~ radiology/pathology services whether inpatient or outpatient
  - ~ treatment of mental illness — limited payments
  - ~ x-rays including portable x-rays in your home
  - ~ services of your doctor's office nurse
  - ~ drugs and biologicals that cannot be self-administered
  - ~ transfusions of blood and blood components
  - ~ medical supplies
  - ~ physical/occupational therapy and speech pathology services

Chiropractors
• Manipulation of spine to correct subluxation (dislocation demonstrated by x-ray)

Podiatrists
• Treatment or injuries of the foot (hammer toe, bunion deformities, heel spurs, etc.)
• Not routine foot care

Dentists
• Medical problems more extensive than teeth or structures directly supporting the teeth
• Hospital stay for severe or complicated dental procedures, even if procedure is not covered
• Not routine care (extractions, fillings, root canals, etc.)

Optometrists
• Cataract spectacles
• Contact lenses
• Intra-ocular lenses after cataract surgery
• Not routine eye exams or eyeglasses

Outpatient hospital services covered
• Emergency room/outpatient clinic, including same-day surgery
• Laboratory tests billed by hospital
• Mental health services in a partial hospitalization psychiatric program
  ~ physician must certify inpatient treatment would be required without it
• X-rays and other radiology services
• Medical supplies (splints, casts, etc.)
• Drugs/biologicals that cannot be self-administered

Home Health Services: (Must meet all three criteria)
• Medical doctor prescribes
• Doctor or therapist sets up treatment
• Doctor periodically reviews plan
  ~ if you have Part A and B, then Part A pays for some home health services
  ~ if you have only Part B, then Part B pays
  ~ outpatient physical and occupational therapy
  ~ speech pathology services

Special Practitioners
• Must be approved and accept assignment
• Certified registered nurse anaesthetist
• Certified nurse midwife
• Clinical psychologist
• Clinical social worker
• Physician assistant
• Nurse practitioner/clinical nurse specialist in collaboration with physician

Comprehensive Outpatient Rehabilitation Facility (CORF)
• Referred by physician who certifies need
• Services include:
 ~ physician
 ~ physical/speech/occupational/respiratory therapy
 ~ counselling
 ~ related services

Partial Hospitalization For Mental Health "Day Treatment"
• Provided by hospital outpatient department
• Provided by community mental health center

Rural Health Clinics
• Basically same services provided under *covered* services
• Certain laboratory tests

Federally-qualified health centers
• Basically same services provided under *covered* services
• X-rays, canes and crutches, etc.
• Certain laboratory tests
 ~ exempt from annual deductible

Laboratory Services
• 100% of approved charges
• Must participate in Medicare
• Must accept assignment
• Must be approved for specific test

Pap Smear
• Screens for cervical cancer
• Once every three years
• More often for high-risk patients
• Diagnostic Pap smears when symptoms are present

Mammography (Breast cancer screen)
• X-ray screenings
• Every 24 months
• For additional information, call 1-800-4-CANCER

Kidney Dialysis And Transplants
• For specific information contact
    Consumer Information Centre
    Department 33
    Pueblo, Colorado 81009
    Booklet 594B

Heart And Liver Transplants
• Under certain limited conditions
• Contact Medicare carrier

Outpatient Mental Health Treatment Limitation
• 50% of approved amount

Services Not Covered
• Services performed by relatives or members of same household
• Services which other government programs pay for
• Custodial care when that is the *only* care needed
  ~ daily living help which allows patient to remain in own home, yet can
    be provided by non- professionals
  ~ care provided in nursing homes for chronic, long-term illnesses and disabilities
• Care not reasonable/necessary under Medicare standards
  ~ drugs/devices not approved by FDA
  ~ medical procedures/services performed using experimental procedures
  ~ services, drugs, devices not considered safe because they are
    experimental or investigational
  ~ hospital or skilled nursing facility when care could have been provided
    elsewhere (home/outpatient) even if doctor admitted
  ~ days spent in hospital/skilled facility longer than necessary
  ~ extra practitioner visits
• Routine physical examinations and related tests
• Eye examinations for eyeglasses
• Ear examinations for hearing aids
• Prescription drugs
• Routine foot care
• Blood transfusions, outpatient basis
• Cosmetic surgery, unless needed due to accidental injury to improve
  function of malformed body part
• Outpatient physical/occupational/speech therapy
• Care outside the United States excluding, Puerto Rico, U. S. Virgin Islands,
  Guam, American Samoa, and Northern Mariana Islands

May pay for inpatient hospital services received in Canada or Mexico:
• If you are in the U. S. when medical emergency occurs and Canadian/Mexican
  hospital is closer than a U. S. hospital that can treat the emergency
• If you are travelling through Canada without unreasonable delay when medical
  emergency occurs and Canadian hospital is closest
• If you live in U. S., yet Canadian/Mexican hospital is closer than nearest
  U. S. hospital that can treat the medical condition, even if there is no emergency
• Doctor/ambulance services furnished by Canada/Mexico in connection with covered
  hospital stay

Normally you are not responsible for claims submitted, yet denied for the following:
• The service was unreasonable and unnecessary
• healthcare provider did not comply with certain federal requirements

BRIEF SUMMARY

MEDICARE PART B: Medical Insurance

Deductible
• $100 per calendar year

Monthly Premium
• $42.50 — may change the first of each year

Co-Insurance
• On assignment — 20% of approved charges
• Not on assignment — 20% plus up to an additional 15% of charges
• Claims must be filed 24 months from date of service

Benefits
• Medical services
  ~ 80% of approved amount after deductible
  ~ doctor's services
  ~ inpatient and outpatient surgical and medical supplies and services
  ~ physical and speech therapy
  ~ diagnostic tests
  ~ durable medical equipment
• Mental health services
  ~ 50% of approved amount for outpatient mental health services
• Outpatient hospital
  ~ 80% of approved amount
  ~ unlimited if deemed medically necessary
  ~ payment is based on hospital costs
  ~ diagnosis and treatment of injury or illness
• Clinical laboratory services
  ~ usually 100% of approved amount
  ~ unlimited if deemed medically necessary
  ~ blood tests
  ~ urinalysis
• Home healthcare services
  ~ usually 100% of approved amount
  ~ intermittent or part-time skilled care
  ~ home health aide
• Durable medical equipment
  ~ 80% of approved amount
• Blood — per calendar year
  ~ 80% of approved amount
  ~ first three pints must be paid for or replaced
  ~ blood paid for or replaced under Part A does not have to be paid for or replaced
  ~ unlimited after first three pints
• Ambulatory surgical services
  ~ 80% of approved amount
  ~ unlimited if deemed medically necessary

HEALTH MANAGEMENT ORGANIZATIONS — HMOs

S: It might be useful for us to talk about (HMOs) Health Management Organizations. HMOs provide coordinated care plans and may offer benefits not covered by Medicare, for little or no additional costs. HMOs often eliminate much of the paperwork involved in medical care. Eligibility for many HMOs requires that you be enrolled in Medicare Part B, and continue to pay Part B premiums, but you would not have to pay Medicare's deductibles or co-insurance amounts.

Most HMOs require that you not be receiving care in a Medicare-certified hospice program, nor have permanent kidney failure. Each plan has its own medical network of doctors, hospitals, skilled care facilities, home health agencies, and other medical providers. You may choose your primary care physician from their list of providers. If you do not choose a primary physician, one will be assigned to you. The primary care physician is responsible for managing your medical care. You would be allowed to change primary care physicians, as long as you choose one that is on the list of providers. Usually you have to live within the HMO's service area, and are required to get all services from the HMO plan. Some HMOs have restrictive enrollment policies and you may be denied coverage for pre-existing conditions. All plans that have contracts with Medicare are required to have an advertised, open enrollment for at least 30 days each calendar year. Once you are enrolled, you may stay in the plan as long as the HMO has a Medicare contract.

Since there are different types of Medicare contracts, you will need to find out if the plan has a *risk,* or *POS* (point-of-service), or *cost* contract with Medicare. Risk plans have lock-in requirements, which means that you are *locked* into receiving all covered medical care through that plan or from referrals made through that plan. Normally, if you receive services not covered under that plan, neither the plan nor Medicare will pay for those services, unless the services are due to an emergency. Under the POS plan you would be permitted to receive certain services outside the plan's network of providers and the plan would pay as much as 80% of the charges. You would be responsible for the remaining 20%.

Cost plans do not have lock-in requirements, which means that you have the option of going to the medical providers within the plan's network, or you could receive treatment from providers outside the plan's network. In that case, the plan would not pay for those services, but Medicare would pay for its share of approved charges. You would then be responsible for Medicare deductibles, premiums, and co-payment amounts, as well as all unapproved charges.

Cost plans may be a good choice for individuals who travel a lot or live outside the plan's area part of the year, because other plans provide coverage for a *fixed period of time* when you travel, therefore, your coverage would be limited to those times, under those plans.

MEDIGAP

S: You may want to consider Medigap, which is a Medicare supplemental insurance policy normally purchased through private insurance companies. It is designed to help pay healthcare expenses either not covered, or not fully-covered, by Medicare. Medigap may also help pay deductibles, premiums, and co-insurance amounts. There is an open enrollment period that begins six months from the date you become enrolled in Medicare Part B. You are then eligible to purchase the Medigap plan of your choice. You cannot be turned down or charged higher premiums, due to poor health, if you buy a Medigap plan during this initial six month period. However, once this Medigap enrollment period ends, you might not be able to purchase the plan of your choice.

You may get a list of names for HMO plans, additional information regarding Medigap, and a free copy of the *Guide to Health Insurance for People with Medicare* by calling a state insurance counselor in your state, or by calling the Health Care Financing Administration.

K: Dr. Haymon, thank you for explaining the differences between Medicare Part A and Medicare Part B, and for helping us to better understand supplemental insurance.

MEDICAID

K: There is still Medicaid. Dr. Haymon, can you help us understand Medicaid?

S: Medicaid is our nation's joint federal and state healthcare program. It not only provides healthcare, but it also provides long-term care coverage to about 32 million elderly people. One of the ways we might distinguish between Medicare and Medicaid is to think of the *Medi* in Medicare as medical, then *care.* When we think of Medicaid, we think of the *Medic* as medical, then *aid.* Similar to Aid to Families with Dependent Children or Aid to Veterans, Medicaid is medical aid for people who cannot afford medical coverage on their own.

Medicaid is based on need. People who qualify for Medicaid live somewhere around the poverty level. Medicaid requires only a minimal cost-sharing contribution from the people who qualify. It's not nearly as costly as Medicare. For example, Medicare Part A has a $736 deduction for every benefit period, plus co-payments. Medicare Part B has an annual deductible of $100, plus co-payments. Medicare remains the same, no matter what state you live in. That's not true for Medicaid. Since Medicaid is a joint venture between the federal and state governments, it varies from state to state. States which have the lowest per capita income get a greater percentage of federal dollars for Medicaid because it is intended for poor people. The federal government usually contributes anywhere from 50% to 80% of every dollar paid out for Medicaid.

K: Does Medicaid pay for both hospitalization and non-hospitalization care?

S: That depends on what state you live in. However, most state Medicaid programs will help pay for some inpatient and outpatient hospital care, including nursing home and some home health assistance. In many states, lab tests and sometimes prescription drugs are covered. In some states, Medicaid will even pay for eyeglasses, hearing aids, rehabilitation and psychological services, medications, and hospice care. Individuals who think they will need Medicaid assistance need to contact their own state Medicaid office.

K: Is there a similar age requirement to qualify for Medicaid, as there is with Medicare? Do you have to be 65 to get Medicaid?

S: No. Remember Medicaid is based on need. About 72% of Medicaid beneficiaries are adults and children from low income families, because they live at the poverty level. Although the elderly and disabled make up only 28% of all of the recipients of Medicaid, this group actually accounts for nearly 60% of all of the spending, due to the use of acute and long-term care. Should you need healthcare or long term care, whether you're old or middle-aged or a child, if you're living near the poverty level you could qualify for Medicaid.

Medicaid for the Medically Needy

Many states offer additional state Medicaid programs, such as Medicaid for the Medically Needy. These programs are designed for people whose income is too high for them to qualify for regular Medicaid, but too low to be able to pay additional medical bills. The assistance provided by these programs is based on a month-to-month need for help in paying medical bills. Some states offer Medicaid expansion programs which provide ongoing Medicaid for individuals with incomes less than 90% of the federal poverty guidelines. And, Kathryn, there are other Medicaid programs provided by some states. Let me tell you about them.

Special Low-Income Medicare Beneficiaries —SLMB's

Your state may also offer programs commonly referred to as SLMB's, Special Low-Income Medicare Beneficiary programs. These programs are designed for individuals whose incomes are between 100% and 110% of the federal poverty guidelines. The purpose of these programs is to help individuals pay the premium for Medicare Part B.

Qualified Medicare Beneficiaries —QMB's

There may also be programs referred to as QMB's, Qualified Medicare Beneficiaries, which provide assistance for individuals unable to pay the deductibles, premiums, and co-insurance amounts required for Medicare Parts A and B. Some states provide for hospice programs for individuals who do not have Medicare.

Institutional Care Programs — ICP's

Some states offer Medicaid programs referred to as ICP's, Institutional Care Programs, which help individuals pay for nursing home care. Some states have programs covered under spousal impoverishment policies that provide assistance to the wife or husband who remains in the community while her or his spouse resides in a care facility. Every state has its own Medicaid programs, therefore, you would need to inquire about assistance within the state where eligibility is being sought.

K: Thank you. Now let's move on to other state programs. Beyond the worlds of Medicare and Medicaid, are there other programs that can be of help?

State Funded Programs

S: There are usually many state funded programs for the elderly and many of those will pay for services not covered by Medicare Part A or B, or by Medicaid.

Optional State Supplemental — OSS

Many states provide programs often referred to as OSS, Optional State Supplemental assistance. The purpose of these programs is to supplement the income of individuals who reside in an adult congregate living facility which accepts state clients, or who live in a foster home, or other specialized living arrangements.

State Supplements — SS

Other states provide what may be referred to as SS, State Supplements. State supplements are customarily intended to be used for room and board and certain other services provided by authorized facilities.

Supplemental Security Income — SSI

Some states offer SSI, Supplemental Security Income, to help individuals who have few assets and low income. This program is designed to assure persons who are 65 or older, disabled, or blind that they have a minimum level of income. This is primarily for people who live below the poverty level. They may apply for SSI benefits and receive a monthly cash amount that will bring them at least up to the poverty level. As with most programs, there are specific eligibility requirements for SSI benefits. Individuals would need to contact their local Social Security office to determine whether or not they qualify. However, as I mentioned earlier, every state has its own specific programs, and individuals would need to contact their Department of Elder Affairs, the Area Agency on Aging, or perhaps the Health and Rehabilitative Services, within their own state.

K: In this time of an elderly person's life, money may be tight. Their income is probably reduced, and everything seems to cost a lot. What are other sources of help?

S: There are several ways to relieve the financial burden for many elderly people.

Food Stamp Program

There is the Food Stamp Program, which is designed to guarantee an adequate diet to individuals who are living on a limited, fixed income. Food stamps are issued free of charge, and age is not a factor. People don't necessarily have to be destitute to get food stamps. I recommend that individuals contact their local Food Stamp office to find out if they qualify.

VETERAN'S ADMINISTRATION

K: What about the Veterans Administration? Does the VA have programs specifically designed for senior citizens?

S: Yes. Some VA benefits include pensions, nursing home care, hospitalization and outpatient medical treatment, as well as disability benefits and services for the blind. VA benefits also customarily pay for prosthetic appliances and a clothing allowance.

K: A clothing allowance?

S: Yes. Individuals who have prosthetic devices that cause their clothes to wear out prematurely, or perhaps the device tears their clothes, could receive an allowance to help replace their worn-out clothes. Alcohol and drug treatment is also provided by the Veterans Administration, as well as life insurance and death benefits for survivors of disabled veterans.

K: When you say, "death benefits," is that revenue from an insurance policy?

S: No. It's burial flags, burial in a national cemetery, a headstone or grave marker, and reimbursement for burial expenses if the veteran dies in a VA medical facility, or if the veteran is receiving VA benefits at the time of her or his death.

K: Does every veteran qualify for these benefits?

S: Not necessarily. Some benefits are available to all veterans, while other benefits are available only to veterans who served during specific periods of time. Individuals who want additional information about eligibility requirements need to contact the Veterans Administration office.

FEDERAL INCOME TAX

K: They say only two things are inevitable, death and taxes. I suppose this would be a place to talk about taxes. Is there help for elderly people who can't fill out their income tax forms?

S: Yes. If people need help in filling out their income tax forms, they may contact the Internal Revenue Service or the American Association of Retired Persons, the AARP, in their area.

K: Are there certain tax exemptions for elderly people?

S: Yes. In addition to personal exemptions, individuals 65 or older are eligible for an additional deduction. If they are blind, they are eligible for yet a third deduction. Persons 55 or older, who sell their primary residence, are presently entitled to a one-time exclusion of up to $125,000 of the gain realized on the sale of their property.

K: Are there any special requirements for this deduction?

S: Normally, the person must have lived in the house for at least three of the last five years, but that's not always the case.

K: What about income from Social Security and other benefits? Do elderly people have to pay tax on that income?

S: Not usually. Income from Social Security, Supplemental Security Income, and certain other public assistance programs customarily is not taxable. However, it depends on the individual's total income. Therefore, I would suggest that you check with the IRS for clarification on that.

INDIVIDUAL RETIREMENT ACCOUNTS (IRA's)

K: What do we need to know about individual pension and retirement plans?

S: Individual retirement accounts, IRA's, are common. Individuals are normally allowed to make contributions until they are 70 years old and taxes are deferred on those contributions until they start drawing the money out. However, when an individual reaches 70, she or he must start drawing money out of her or his IRA account. They also have to start paying taxes on it at that time.

When you're trying to get organized and help your parents get all of their finances in order, and you're trying to get all of the legal documents and the advance directives, and you're trying to go through all of the old purses and shoes, you might want to ask your folks if they have an IRA, or if they have other investments. If they have dealt with a stock broker, find out who and with what company. Far too often, what happens is the elderly person will have a stroke or some other accident and then one of two things might happen, either their memory is gone and they don't even remember that they had the account, or where it is, or maybe their ability to speak or write is gone and they can't tell you, even if they do remember. It is very important that you talk with your parents and find out all that you can before a crisis happens.

Every year there are probably hundreds of thousands of dollars, maybe even millions of dollars, that go unclaimed simply because families did not know their elderly loved ones had money in certain accounts or certain retirement funds. It is important to check with every employer your mom or dad worked for to find out if there were any savings plans or any type of retirement benefits.

Property Tax Reductions

K: Dr. Haymon, I have also heard there are special reductions on property taxes for elderly people?

S: In many states, elderly people have the benefit of paying reduced taxes on their property. Most states offer a homestead exemption that allows the home-owner to deduct some pre-determined amount from the taxable value of her or his home. Some states allow exemptions for disabled persons, veterans, and for widows and widowers. Many states completely exempt persons with certain disabilities from paying any property taxes at all. For example, persons who are legally blind, confined to a wheelchair, paraplegic, or quadriplegic, may be totally exempt from property taxes in some states. In order to determine if individuals are receiving all of the exemptions they are entitled to, you would need to contact a tax appraiser's office. Those are usually listed in the white pages of most telephone directories and are probably under County listings.

Reverse Mortgages

K: What if a senior citizen owns her or his own home, but doesn't have enough money to pay the water bill, the phone bill, or that kind of thing? Is there a way that person can stay in their home and still generate money or capital?

S: Yes. For individuals who want to remain in their own home, but really can't afford to live in it because they can't afford utility bills, repairs, or upkeep, many banks offer reverse mortgages. Those are very similar to normal mortgages, except in reverse. Normally, the home has to be completely paid for, or almost so; there has to be a lot of equity in the house. The person would actually borrow money on her or his own home and receive a certain amount of money per month. That amount would be deducted from the equity in the house. They might set it up for 10 or 15 years, or they might decide they will need another $1,000 or so each month until they die.

K: Sounds like that could be an answer for some people.

S: It is an answer, but I do have a word of caution here. Eligibility for some government programs, such as Supplemental Security Income, Food Stamps, Medicaid, and other programs, might be affected if the person has a reverse mortgage. The income from a reverse mortgage increases their monthly income, therefore, they might not be eligible for certain programs. If you are already receiving benefits, or if you think you might need Medicaid in the very near future, I would at least check with those agencies to find out what affect, if any, having a reverse mortgage would have on being eligible for those programs.

K: **In other words, it's never simple?**

S: No, it isn't.

K: **Dr. Haymon, thank you so much for all this information. You have truly helped me understand these assistance programs.**

Chapter 7

EMOTIONAL ISSUES

K: **Dr. Haymon, the choices are overwhelming. I can't even imagine the emotional issues — the emotional impact — on a person caring for her or his parents. Could you talk to us about that?**

S: Yes, Kathryn, but first I feel this topic also needs a disclaimer. Please allow me to say, human emotions vary from person to person and are always complex. All too often, people think they *should* or *should not* feel certain feelings, or that some feelings are unacceptable. A common assumption is, no one could possibly understand what they are feeling. It may be that we can never truly understand what another is feeling, however, there are common emotions, such as anger, guilt, grief, helplessness and general feelings of being overwhelmed, which accompany the responsibility of caring for an aging loved one. All emotions are acceptable, and we need to acknowledge our feelings. Not only do our emotions influence the decisions we make, but certain emotions may be so overwhelming that we become immobilized and are unable to make any decision at all. I have personally felt all these emotions, as well as learned the consequences of denying some of them. Besides the emotions of anger, guilt, grief and feelings of being overwhelmed, resentment, sadness, and depression may also be felt, as well as feelings on the other side of the coin. You may feel honored, privileged and helpful. All of these feelings are acceptable and normal. It is also common for individuals to have mixed feelings or to bounce from one feeling to another. Caregivers who start with mixed feelings about their parents or other loved ones may experience extreme discomfort created by internal struggles.

K: **What do you mean by that?**

S: You might be torn between loving your parents, yet disliking them at the same time. You may also harbor unresolved childhood feelings of anger and resentment. It may be that a loved one abused you or was not there for you. You might want your loved one to come and live with you, and at the same time, you know this would not be the best decision for your family. You might also be torn between what you think is best and a different opinion from your spouse or some other family member. You may vacillate between what you want to do and what you think members of society expect you to do. You may have made some previous commitments to your loved ones but now, due to a change in circumstances, you are no longer in a position to fulfill these commitments. These feelings are not unusual. Feelings are neither good nor bad. Feelings do not have to be acted upon. Feelings just simply are. It is important, however, to acknowledge your feelings, since feelings affect judgement and therefore influence decisions you might make. However, before individuals can truly acknowledge and accept their feelings, they must first identify them. It might be helpful to remember feelings are usually identified with just one word.

> Besides the emotions of anger, guilt, grief and feelings of being overwhelmed, resentment, sadness, and depression may also be felt, as well as feelings on the other side of the coin.

K: What do you mean, one word?

S: If you tell me you feel like running down the hall screaming, I won't have a clue as to how you feel because you have just described a behavior, not a feeling. I won't know if you are running down the hall screaming because you are afraid, or angry, or happy. Maybe you just won the lottery.

K: I see.

S: It's also important to accurately label whatever the feeling is. Here is a technique I use when I am trying to determine exactly what I am feeling. I close my eyes and locate where I'm experiencing the feeling in my body. With my eyes still closed, I try to see the color of the feeling. Then, when I've isolated the feeling, I give it a name. I complete the sentence, "I feel _____." Only one word. "I feel *sad*." "I feel *happy*." "I feel *angry*." "I feel *guilty*." "I feel *depressed*." Do you see what I mean?

K: What about the negative feelings?

S: Unfortunately, there are certain feelings that are often categorized as negative. Those seem to be the ones which cause individuals the most conflict and are most often viewed as unacceptable. Anger is one of those feelings. However, it is normal to feel angry when faced with the responsibility of providing care for an elderly loved one.

K: What would I be angry about?

S: I will let you try out some of the most common responses I've heard: Angry that you have to be the caregiver; angry at the situation; angry that this has happened to you; angry that others do not help; angry that there are not other choices; angry that healthcare is so expensive; angry that you don't have more money; angry that you are left to make decisions that your loved ones could have made for themselves years ago.

Other people have reported that they feel angry because there are so many decisions to be made, angry with their loved ones for their irritating behaviors and their lack of gratitude. Some people are angry because it seems that no matter how much they do, it is never enough and never good enough. Sometimes they are angry with their spouses or other family members because they seem to add to their stress. Some have reported getting angry with their bosses and others because they don't understand when they have to be away from their jobs to tend their parents. It is not uncommon to be angry with doctors and other professionals. Some people are angry with God. Sometimes we are angry with ourselves because we didn't anticipate this day and plan better for it. Sometimes we are angry with ourselves for being angry. And sometimes we are angry and don't even know why we are angry.

K: Is there anything good at all about anger?

S: One of the things I've learned about anger is that by acknowledging anger people are usually empowered to make decisions and take action. However, anger can also be destructive by manifesting in bodily symptoms, as well as blocking creative energy. Anger can also be destructive to other people as a result of hurtful words and harmful behaviors. Anger can also separate us from other people who might be able to help us.

It might be useful to note that anger is one layer up from fear. If we look underneath our anger to see what is driving it, we often come face-to-face with our fears. Sometimes, underneath our anger regarding taking care of elderly relatives, lie many fears. We fear we will make wrong decisions, we will not do it right, other people will criticize us. Sometimes, under our anger is fear about our own death. When our parents die, our generation is next. That's a very frightening thought for some people, and rather than deal with their fear, many people find it easier to address their anger. In some ways, society accepts anger more readily than fear. Many of us were taught not to be afraid, or at least not to let anybody know when we were afraid. We need to acknowledge our anger and our fear and deal with them.

> ...anger may also be destructive by manifesting in bodily symptoms, as well as blocking creative energy.

K: What do you mean by deal with them ?

S: One way is to accept whatever you are feeling without placing any value judgement on it. When you feel angry or afraid, don't just simply say to yourself, or think to yourself, "I'm angry," or "I'm afraid," say it out loud. It makes a tremendous difference when we are open and honest about our feelings. So you might say, "I'm angry and it's okay that I'm angry."

K: Say it out loud?

S: Say it out loud. Say, "I'm afraid and it's okay that I'm afraid." One of the ways I dealt with my feelings was to talk about whatever I was feeling with a close friend. Although I wasn't necessarily looking for advice, it was extremely helpful to have someone to just talk with about these feelings. There is great therapeutic value in talking about our emotions. I strongly recommend that you talk about your feelings with a close friend, relative, counselor, member of the clergy, or perhaps someone else in a similar situation, but talk about whatever you are feeling.

K: What are some other ways people can handle these emotions?

S: You may try whatever you have used in the past to cope with anger and frustration, whether it be cleaning out a closet or exercising. For some people, it is deep breathing or meditating, going for a walk, chopping wood, gardening, or taking a relaxing bath. Whatever has worked in the past, that's what I recommend people use. The important thing is to take care of yourself.

K: Dr. Haymon, you mentioned helplessness as one of the feelings commonly experienced by caregivers. Help us understand how the caregiver is the one feeling so helpless.

S: Helplessness is another one of those feelings many commonly view as negative and unacceptable. It is common for individuals to feel helpless, incompetent, powerless and overwhelmed. Sometimes we feel out-of-control when we are dealing with the responsibilities of taking care of an elderly relative. These feelings can be demoralizing and may be exaggerated when we are in the midst of a pile of bureaucratic forms. I can tell you there are lots of bureaucratic forms. Those feelings are sometimes exaggerated when we are tired or when we have other major stressors. The other areas in our life continue, even though we have the responsibility of taking care of our parents. Feelings of helplessness are also intensified when we seem unable to find doctors or other professionals who understand our problems. Often, feelings of helplessness are associated with feeling totally out-of-control. Often, when we feel overwhelmed, it is because we are attempting to look at and handle everything at once.

> Feelings of helplessness are also intensified when we seem unable to find doctors or other professionals who understand our problems.

K: How can we deal with feeling overwhelmed?

S: There are several things you might do to manage these feelings. First, admit your feelings. Admit you feel overwhelmed, then stop and make two lists. On the first list, write down the three most important tasks you feel you need to accomplish that pertain to your caregiving role. Put them in order of importance. Only put three on this first list. On the second list, write down several small things that can be handled relatively easily or within a short period of time. Next, decide to whom you can delegate some of these tasks, from either list or from both lists. Then do exactly that. Delegate these things. For example, on a typical day for me, I might need to take one or both of my parents to a doctor, complete medical and insurance forms, do their laundry, shop for their groceries, go to the pharmacy, tidy their house and feed their pets. Those were just a few of the things I had to do for them. Of course, this was all in addition to my already full schedule of things I had to do in my own life. I was working a 50-hour week. You may be surprised to learn that a friend or a relative will be glad to pick up grocery items while they are doing their own shopping. Maybe a neighbor wouldn't mind feeding their pets, which might save you a trip across town. Maybe there's a transportation service that would safely transport your parents to the doctor. Many of us are not accustomed to asking other people to help, but I can assure you there are many people who would be more than willing to help. Remember to take care of yourself. Caring for aging loved ones could go on for a decade or more. The last thing you want to do is burn yourself out.

> ...on a typical day for me, I might need to take one or both of my parents to a doctor, complete medical and insurance forms, do their laundry, shop for their groceries, go to the pharmacy, tidy their house and feed their pets.

K: How about those of us who can't delegate, who say, "Nobody can do it as well as I can?"

S: It is true. You probably could handle any and all the tasks better than anyone else could, but as long as things get taken care of, consider them done. This will allow you to narrow your focus and therefore channel your energy. We might think about this in terms of a flood light. Flood lights spread light over a large area, but the light gets dimmer the farther away from the bulb you get. Now let's think about narrowing the focus of that same amount of light and channeling that energy into a laser beam. I want you to think about how much more powerful the light is when it is that focused. It is the same way with our own energy. When we focus and channel our energy in one direction, we are a lot more powerful than when we spread ourselves so thin.

K: That certainly makes sense, but what if you can't find anyone to delegate these things to?

S: If anything is left on either list, then you decide which ones you will do and in what order you will do them. Later, should you find yourself getting anxious because something has not been done, stop and ask yourself two questions. Remember there are two lists and here are two questions: What is the worst thing that will happen if I don't get this done today? What is the worst thing that will happen if I never get this done? You might be surprised to learn that nothing awful will happen either way. The truth is, most things are only important because we have assigned importance to them. It is my opinion that few things are important at all and probably nothing is important enough to be allowed to rob you of your peace and sense of well-being. You cannot live tomorrow today, nor change the past. Remind yourself that you are only one person and you will do what you can. Then let go of any regrets that you have about yesterday, or worries you might have about tomorrow. Regret and worry only rob us of our peace and needed energy. So when you feel powerless, helpless, overwhelmed, or out-of-control, pause for reflection and applaud yourself for all the things you have already tolerated and all the things you have already taken care of.

K: That is really good advice. What about guilt? I would imagine there is a great amount of guilt associated with all of this

S: Yes. Guilt is yet another emotion that seems to create conflict for many individuals, and it is quite common for caregivers to feel guilty. You may feel guilty for the way you have behaved towards your parents in the past; guilty about your thoughts and feelings; guilty for allowing the elderly person to come live with you and interrupt the lives of other family members.

You may feel guilty about placing your loved ones in a nursing home and not allowing them to come live with you. You may feel guilty that you have to work and you can't stay home and take care of them. You may feel guilty for spending time with your family and friends, instead of spending time with your elderly parents, because "they might not have much time left;" guilty for spending time with them and away from your spouse and children; guilty for making promises that you can no longer keep; guilty for wishing that you did not have to care for them. Some people report they feel guilty about their parents' illnesses, even though they know it's not their fault and there is nothing they can do about it.

> You may feel guilty that you have to work and you can't stay home and take care of them.

I felt guilty about the decision to take away their independence, especially when I had to ask Carl for his truck keys. Sometimes, we feel guilty that they can no longer live alone; guilty they can no longer drive themselves; guilty that we continue with our own lives and have health and happiness, and they don't. Sometimes, just as with anger, we feel guilty and we don't even know why we feel guilty.

K: You mentioned scattered families. Some of us who live long distances from our parents are under particular guilt. Is it worse for us?

S: I don't know the research on that, but it does appear guilt may be greater for some families that are geographically separated from their loved ones, because they feel guilty they are not there to see them more often and take care of them.

K: I know it makes us feel bad, but what's wrong with feeling guilty? It seems so normal

S: The primary problem with guilt, as with other emotions, occurs when feelings are not recognized for what they are. When that happens, feelings may destructively influence our judgement, and our judgement affects decisions we may make. It is also interesting to note that there is often a *should* command that undergirds each guilt feeling. When we use the word, *should*, it implies there was one, perfect way and we failed to utilize it. Consequently, people sometimes feel guilty because they are not perfect and their parents were not perfect. It's only when we realize there is no "perfect" that we may realize there is no reason to feel guilty. There is no one, perfect way to do, or to have done, anything. As a matter of fact, there is an infinite number of ways to do most things. When you recognize you are feeling guilty, try to identify the *should* statement. When you catch yourself thinking or saying, "I should have," or, "They should have," replace the "should have" with "could have." By changing the "should" to "could," we are able to transform self-punishment for not having lived up to some internal standard, into sound problem-solving and decision-making.

> There is no one, perfect way to do, or to have done, anything.

K: This has been helpful, because I have an older parent and I am constantly saying to myself, "I really should have mother come and live with us," and I leave it at that. Then I feel terribly guilty that I don't. If I say she could come and live with us, what's the difference? Walk me through that. How would that help me get out of the guilt mode?

S: Okay, let's talk about that for a minute. When you say you really *should* have your mother come and live with you, that implies there is a perfect way, and the perfect way is to have your mother come and live with you. You can change that and say, " I *could* have my mother come and live with me, and if I did, what are the things I would need to consider, and would that be the very best decision?" Then you go through a decision-making process. Remember, when we change *should* to *could,* it changes internal self-punishment into problem-solving and decision-making. So when you walk that through, you say, "I could have my mother come live with me; now let me look around. Would my house be safe for her? Would there be someone home with her to take care of her?" You go through a decision-making process.

K: That's great, because I would say, "Would she have someone to play bridge with? Would the town be as much fun as where she lives? Would she trip on the stairs, because we have many stairs? Would she like it?" You have really helped me here, because I am suddenly giving up some guilt about where she lives, rather

than what I think I should do. Thank you, that's really helpful

S: Thank you for the example

K: But, Dr. Haymon, how about the old saying, "Hindsight is 20/20?" I think, when most of us look back at situations, we see things so much more clearly.

S: Of course I've heard that old saying, but Kathryn, that too implies accuracy. I'm not sure that when I look back on events I see them with any greater accuracy than I did during the time I was experiencing them. I only know I see them differently, which may or may not be more accurate. Unfortunately, feeling guilty tends to keep us looking for ways to correct the past and make it *perfect*, instead of letting it go and just accepting whatever the past was. There is no way to relive your childhood. There is no way to undo anything that occurred in the past. Maybe you never liked your parents. Some people even hated their parents. There is no way to remedy that. Decisions and plans now need to be based on what seems best for all concerned. This is not the time to play "get even." This is the time to be honest with yourself.

> You might find that little things make you sad, or you feel like crying for no apparent reason.

K: What do you mean by being honest with yourself?

S: If there is something you believe you need to apologize to your loved ones for, then do so. If they are coherent enough to understand, that's great. Even if they can't understand, for whatever reason, apologize anyway. You see, the apology is more for your benefit than it is for theirs. If your parents are still mentally competent enough for you to talk with them, and there are things unresolved you feel need to be addressed, then by all means, talk with them. You have a lot to gain from this. However, don't expect them to have the same need to clear the air that you do. Often, things we hold vividly in our own memories have long since been forgotten by others. So to expect that someone else will remember things in the same light you do is to set yourself up for possible hurt and disappointment.

K: You say grief is another common feeling. Are you talking about when our parents die?

S: Kathryn, a lot of people believe the only time we feel grief is when someone passes away. However, as our loved ones age, their health declines, or they lose their faculties, there are many losses to grieve. Sometimes we grieve the loss of a parent, the loss of a companion, the loss of a relationship that was important to us. Sometimes we grieve for the way they used to be and for those qualities that identified who they were. You may grieve for the lost opportunity to have the parents you always wanted, yet you never had, and now realize you never will have. Sometimes, our grief is over what might have been, rather than what really was, because sometimes, what really was, wasn't that great. Whatever our sense of loss, grief is a natural response to loss and we need to grieve our losses.

K: Dr. Haymon, isn't it harder for us to identify grief? I mean, it usually seems clear when we are angry. Now I can listen for the "should" statements when I feel guilty, but I'm not sure I know when I am actually grieving.

S: You might find that little things make you sad, or you feel like crying for no apparent reason. Those feelings of sadness are often intensified by fatigue and sometimes that leads to depression. Grief is an interesting emotion. When it follows death, it may be overwhelming in the beginning, then lessen over time. However, grief associated with irreversible conditions such as dementia, Alzheimer's disease, or kidney failure, seems to go on and on. It shifts back and forth among hope, anger, sadness and grief, and it bounces back and forth. Then, just when you think you have adjusted and are coping, the person's condition may change and you have to go through the grieving process all over again. For example, when I had to place my parents in an assisted living facility, I grieved many losses. I had a laundry list of things I had to grieve. Slowly, I adapted to our new roles. Just when I thought I had adjusted and was coping, they got worse and I had to go through the grieving process all over again.

Another thing is, grief which follows death seems to be understood and accepted by society, yet grief associated with chronic illness is often misunderstood by people who are not close to the person. Many caregivers report their feelings of sadness worsen as they watch their loved ones suffer as their illness progresses. It is not uncommon to think your loved ones might actually be better off if they died so they wouldn't have to suffer anymore.

I want to stress again that caring for aging loved ones can last for years. We need to give ourselves permission to have a meaningful life outside of our caregiving role. It helps if you understand that caregiving for an aging parent is

> It is not uncommon to think your loved ones might actually be better off if they died so they wouldn't have to suffer anymore.

part of your life, but it is not your entire life. We need to give our caretaking responsibilities appropriate attention, but we don't need to allow them to consume us. Taking care of elderly people is like running a marathon, and I have done that. You have to pace yourself, or you will never make it to the finish line. I cannot tell you the number of women I have talked to, all of whom had spent over 10 years taking care of one or both parents, and they literally burned themselves out in the process. One of them was hospitalized for exhaustion. Another had spent so much time and energy on caring for her parents that her husband left. When she came out of the process and looked around, she was totally alone. Yet another was grieving the fact she had missed so much of her own children's lives because she was so focused on her mother. The point is, when you put on the caregiver hat, you may be wearing it for a long time. You still have other hats, so be sure to wear them, too.

K: **What are some of things we can do to prevent it from consuming our lives?**

S: One of the first things is to schedule downtime for yourself. Most of us already had more on our plates than we could say grace over, before we inherited the responsibility of taking care of an elderly person. So accept the fact that some of the things you used to do on a regular basis will now have to go undone. By all means, don't try to continue doing all the things you were previously doing and squeeze in these additional responsibilities. To do so would probably mean you would have to neglect your own health and well-being. The strain of this could also harm primary relationships. When you are feeling frustrated because you can no longer keep your house as clean as you once did, or your yard no longer gets "Yard of the Month," and you are feeling guilty that your family is once again eating fast food, just stop and ask yourself, "What's important here?" It very well may be that your family would rather have a rested, happy person than a home-cooked meal, or "Yard of the Month" sign on the front lawn. Long-term caregiving requires enormous amounts of physical and emotional energy. Since the mind and body are inter-connected, you need to be sure you take care of both. You must do whatever it takes to maintain your own physical and mental health so you don't become depressed, which often happens during the grieving process.

> ...the caregiver was three times more likely to report symptoms of depression than the elderly person she was caring for...

K: **I bet a lot of people get depressed while caring for an elderly relative.**

S: A two-year study at the University of Michigan School of Nursing reported the caregiver was three times more likely to report symptoms of depression than the elderly person she was caring for, and four times more likely to report anger.

K: **Is depression different from being sad?**

S: Depression goes beyond appropriate feelings of sadness. When people become depressed, they often feel discouraged, hopeless, and may have general feelings of despair. In severe cases, depressed individuals report feeling suicidal. Depression is commonly associated with long-term caregiving. Therefore, I would caution you to be aware of the emotional and physical symptoms of depression.

K: **What are some of those symptoms?**

S: It is common for people who are depressed to feel tired. Many experience extreme fatigue, beyond normal tiredness that comes from loss of sleep and rest. Depressed individuals often report feeling restless, anxious, or nervous most of the time. They may spend unusual amounts of time worrying.

Depressed individuals may behave in ways which are abnormal for them. They may have a temper outburst over a minor incident, or be given to mood swings from euphoria to melancholy. They may become overly sensitive, not only to verbal interactions with other people, but overly sensitive to light, noise, and temperature. Depressed persons may have difficulty concentrating. They may experience forgetfulness and loss of short-term memory. Sometimes, people who are depressed say that they think they are losing their minds. In addition to all of that, when individuals are depressed, they may overeat or have no appetite at all. They may oversleep or have bouts of insomnia. What's more, people who are depressed often begin to experience illnesses. Even people who have almost never been sick in the past develop physical symptoms such as headaches, allergies, backaches, gastrointestinal problems, shortness of breath, chest pain, dizziness, ulcers, stomach aches, frequent colds, nervous tics, just to name a few of the ways depression may manifest physically. It is also common for people who are depressed to lose their desire for sex.

K: So what should you do if you think you are depressed?

S: Because depression is so painful, many individuals attempt to self-medicate. In attempts to reduce the anguish of depression, it is common for depressed people to drink more coffee, start smoking again when they had quit for years, or maybe increase the number of cigarettes they smoke every day. It is also common for depressed people to attempt to self-medicate by using alcohol, sleeping pills, tranquilizers or other drugs that increase fatigue by depleting what little precious energy they have left. Many of these substances are themselves depressants. Consequently, they contribute to the depression. They actually make it worse. I encourage people to see their own physician, and to schedule regular checkups. Sometimes, hidden problems such as anemia, high or low blood pressure, or chronic, low-grade infections can contribute to our fatigue level and rob us of much-needed energy. I also encourage people to see a counselor if they think they are depressed. While counseling cannot remove the reason for your depression, it might enable you to deal with it by helping you to sort out your problems and face them one at a time. However, whether you seek professional help, or you simply talk to a friend, relative, or maybe a member of the clergy, talk about your situation with someone. None of these individuals may be able to do one thing about your problem, except to listen to you, but that may be all that they need to do. Sometimes, we can't see the forest for the trees, so sharing our problems with others may give us a chance to see our problems from a whole different perspective, as well as offer us some possible alternatives that maybe we had not even thought of.

> ...people who are depressed often begin to experience illnesses.

K: What about support groups?

S: This is especially true of support groups. It may be that you are not the type to talk in groups, especially not to strangers. Many of us do not want to, as my grandmother used to say, "air our dirty laundry in front of strangers." That's okay, go anyway. It may be comforting just to be with others who can truly relate to what you're going through. Even if you don't want to talk, go and listen. Often, other people in the group have already gone through some of the trials you may presently be going through, and they will be happy to share what has worked and what has not worked for them. These suggestions may save you enormous amounts of time, energy, and money. So while you may think you are not the type to join a group, or that you can't afford the time to attend a group, it may very well be that you cannot afford not to. Once again, you need to schedule time to talk about your situation with someone on a regular basis. There is tremendous benefit that comes from just talking. Talking truly seems to be the oil that soothes the soul. Right now, call up that special friend and set a date to get together and just talk. Make it a weekly date, and no matter what comes up, you keep that date every week. My special friend and I scheduled dinner together every Monday night. She allowed me to vent about my situation with Mother and Carl for half the evening, then I listened to her frustrations for the second half.

> Carl remained unaware of what had happened. He just sat there and watched the movie.

K: So what are some of the other things we should do to take care of ourselves during this time?

S: When the need to provide care continues for years, and you think there is not enough of you to go around, stop and think of ways in which you have been neglecting yourself. One of the first things to go, besides sleep, is proper nutrition. It is vital that you eat well-balanced meals regularly. There are lots of other things you can do to take care of yourself. If you are unable to have quiet time at home, then go to a movie, even if you have to take children or parents with you. Chances are, they will be preoccupied for that couple of hours and you can either escape into the movie, sleep, or just sit there and rest. Now might be a good time for me to tell another true story.

I guess it was about a year and a half ago that I decided to take my mother and stepfather to a movie. I also wanted to spend some time with my little five-year-old friend who lived next door to me. So I was going to take all of them to see The Lion King. Well, I planned an additional half hour because my parents walk very slowly and it takes time to get them in and out of the car. So I allowed time for that. I was so proud of all of us. We made it into the movie. We were in there on time. There was not even an incident. Well, about halfway through the movie, Carl had fallen asleep and he started snoring loudly. My little five-year-old friend started giggling, so I gently shook

Carl to wake him up and to stop the noise that was now disturbing other people. Well, he woke up and let out this loud yawn that seemed to go on for a full minute. At first I was embarrassed, then I was concerned as to what the other people around us must be thinking. To my relief — I guess I was relieved — other people started laughing. Their laughter prompted my laughter and my little friend was still giggling. For the most part, many of us missed the next two or three minutes of The Lion King. Carl remained unaware of what had happened. He just sat there and watched the movie.

> **The process of care-giving could go on for 10 or 15 years, so we need to take care of ourselves.**

K: Did he like it?

S: I am not sure he even remembered seeing it by the time we had gotten out. Needless to say, I sat there until all the lights were on and everybody had left the theater before I got Mother, Carl and my little friend and left.

K: Well it's good to know things like that even happen to the doctors of psychology. Everyone else can get through it, too, I'm sure. Dr. Haymon, I've heard exercise is important as well.

S: Kathryn, exercise is extremely important. At the point when you think you don't have enough time to exercise, that is just the time you need to most. Many caregivers report feeling guilty about taking time for themselves to exercise. They say to themselves, "I should be doing something else." Be mindful of one clear and simple fact: The more you exercise, the more energy you will have. Consequently, you will be able to do other things more efficiently, because exercise will provide enough energy to save you time.

K: I particularly have liked the substituting of *could* for *should*. That has been great advice, but could you recap everything for us?

S: Sure. Caring for elderly loved ones is an emotional time. The emotional roller coaster will probably include anger, guilt, resentment, sadness, depression, feelings of helplessness and being overwhelmed. That roller coaster might also include feelings of honor, privilege, acceptance and hopefulness. We need to remember to acknowledge our feelings, without placing any value judgement on them, and to identify our feelings with one word. Remember, feelings are neither good nor bad, nor do they have to be acted on. The process of caregiving could go on for 10 or 15 years, so we need to take care of ourselves. Schedule downtime, eat properly, exercise, get plenty of rest, have regular physical checkups and, by all means, talk about your feelings. I know I have said that in every section, but it is important. Schedule time every week to talk with a friend, relative or someone about what you are going through. You might need to tell them up front that you are not looking for advice, you just want to vent. Then they won't feel they have to help you fix it.

K: Now that we have looked at the emotional issues for the caregiver, could you address the emotional issues for elderly persons?

S: Kathryn, the transition from independence to dependence is often excruciating. Elderly people report many fears, which include the fear of death, fear of losing everything they have worked for, and fear of not having enough money to sustain them. Some talk about their fear of losing their physical and mental faculties. Others talk about their fear of pain and debilitating illnesses. In addition to their fears, many elderly people tend to worry about many things.

K: For example?

S: They worry about being a burden to their children and other relatives. They worry about what will happen to their spouse if they should die. They worry about what will happen to them if their spouse dies. These are all real and valid fears that often evoke tremendous pain. In order to avoid this emotional trauma, sometimes elderly people stay in denial and cling to their belief that they can still take care of themselves. As we said earlier, denial serves to protect individuals from pain associated with certain realities.

> ...elderly people stay in denial and cling to their belief that they can still take care of themselves.

What I observe with my own folks is that my mother's dementia is so pronounced she doesn't seem concerned about the moment, much less the future. However, Carl moves in and out of contact with reality. During those times when he is lucid and aware of where he is, he expresses nearly all the fears I just talked about. I have sat with him on many occasions when he has cried about being in the nursing home and the realization that he and my mother will never live alone again. I have held him while he cried about not being able to work and provide for my mother. I have also held him as he cried about not being able to drive or even tie his own shoes.

Kathryn, my heart breaks when I see how embarrassed he is over having to wear diapers and needing help to change them. This was once a strong and proud man. He worked hard and paid his taxes. He made a contribution to the world. He enjoyed life, especially driving. My heart aches whenever I see him in so much emotional pain. I am almost thankful when he mentally goes back to a time in his life when he talks about planting crops and feeding the mule and other things he did fifty years ago. It is during those times when he seems to be free of pain. He expresses joy as he talks to me about the crop he just harvested. At times, he maintains the delusion he and my mother will live alone and he will be able to drive his truck again. Some days, Kathryn, he even talks about getting a motorcycle, and this man can hardly stand up without being supported.

K: Dr. Haymon, when your parents talk about things that are totally unreasonable,

like Carl riding a motorcycle, should you try to explain to them that's not possible? Or should you agree with them?

S: That's a very good question. When elderly persons are delusional and operating from an entirely different belief system than we are, there are communication problems. This often creates a double bind for us. On the one hand, if you agree with the delusion, you reinforce it. On the other hand, if you confront it, you drive the delusion deeper.

K: So how do we, as caregivers, find a balance between the two?

S: The important thing is to always show respect for the elderly person. Remember, not too long ago, these individuals were not unlike ourselves. They were independent and managing their own lives, a task many of them have probably done for as long as we have been alive. They deserve respect, understanding and reassurance, even if they had addictions and lived their lives differently than we live ours. The truth is, we all probably do the very best we can just to survive, and these people have survived eighty, ninety, maybe even a hundred years. So if you blatantly tell them they are never going to leave the nursing home, you risk insulting them, as well as creating unnecessary tensions and struggles for them. However, you don't want to be dishonest with them either. So when an elderly person starts talking about leaving the facility or moving back to her or his home, or driving again, just try to remember the purpose of the delusion. That purpose is to protect them from emotional pain. It is very comforting for them to believe in something positive. That's true for all of us.

> I don't confront his delusion by telling him Mother will never be able to take such a trip, and furthermore he will never be able to drive again.

K: So how do you do that? How do you deal with their delusions?

S: One way is to respond to the period in their lives the delusional comments represent. For example, when Carl says something like, "As soon as your mother is better, we are going to take a trip. We'll probably drive all the way to California," I don't confront his delusion by telling him Mother will never be able to take such a trip, and furthermore he will never be able to drive again. I just validate him by responding to that period of time in his life when he was strong, in good health, and independent. So I will say something like, "You really enjoyed the trips you and Mother took a few years back, didn't you?" Now, do you see what I've done? I've responded to the period in his life that his comments represent. I never addressed whether he was actually going to California.

K: So you don't argue with him

S: No, I just encourage him to talk about those times in his life he enjoyed, and soon he has forgotten all about his notion of going to California and he is telling me about the trips he took when he was a young man. Another way to handle delusional comments is to try to keep the person in the present. Instead of responding to what they have said, ask them what they did this morning. Ask them what type of activities they have been involved in. Or here's a really good one, ask them their opinions about something in your own life. Even though you think you wouldn't take any advice they give you, sometimes they surprise you and come up with some very good advice. Indeed, there is a fine line between reinforcing and confronting delusions. However, if you, as a caregiver, will remember to show empathy for the elderly person, tensions and resistance can truly be held to a minimum. This is an emotional time for you; it's an emotional time for your spouse, for your children, and for the elderly person. So I want to encourage people to be patient with themselves and with everyone involved.

> Even though you think you wouldn't take any advice they give you, sometimes they surprise you and come up with some very good advice.

Try to let go of past hurts and focus on the moment. You have been chosen to care for this other human being for a reason. It seems it would be a shame to exchange your time, energy and emotions for anything less than a wonderful opportunity to grow and learn and truly connect with this other person at a level of intimacy that may only be possible through the unselfish motive of simply serving another human being.

K: Dr. Haymon, thank you so much for helping us understand more about our feelings and our parents' feelings as we go through this process of taking care of elderly parents. I am curious about how this will affect a husband or wife.

S: It's not uncommon for the spouse of the caregiver to report confusion as to what his or her role in the caregiving process actually is. Perhaps one of the reasons for this confusion is that there are probably as many different roles as there are caregiving situations. Consequently, there are no right or wrong ways. Let me give you some examples at both ends of this spectrum, with the understanding that there is an infinite number of combinations in between.

The first story was told to me by a friend of mine. I will call him John, but of course that is not his real name. John said his wife, whom I will call Betty, moved her father into their home. Although Betty's father was alcoholic and had been abusive to Betty and her brother and sisters while they were growing up, Betty felt it was her duty to take care of him during his last years. Betty's father had emphysema. He was also on dialysis, which required special meals, as well as trips to the dialysis clinic three times a week. John said he didn't mind Betty's father moving in with them. Their house was certainly large enough to accommodate another person. What he did mind was Betty's attitude during the process of taking care of her father. John told me Betty grew angrier by the day and she vented her anger toward him and their two daughters. Betty was not only angry with her father, she was angry that neither of her three sisters, nor her brother, seemed interested in assuming the responsibility of taking care of him. In addition, they attributed his poor health to his own choices in life, which included smoking heavily and drinking excessively.

Even though they didn't agree with her, Betty's sisters and brother allowed Betty to do whatever she felt she needed to do. Betty could not control her sisters and brother and make them share in providing care for their father. This enraged her. She complained every day. She became more and more unpleasant to be around. Betty started showing signs of depression and became hyper-critical of John, their daughters, and practically everything and everybody around her. John said he and their daughters did everything they could to relieve Betty of her burden.

Consequently, there are no right or wrong ways.

He would take her father to the dialysis clinic and their oldest daughter would bring him home as she returned from school. Soon, he and their daughters were doing virtually all the household chores, the cleaning, the laundry, the cooking. The only thing left for Betty to do was to prepare her father's special meals. No matter how much John and their daughters did, it seemed it was never enough, and never good enough for Betty. She never gave them credit for helping. She continued to complain about how bad she had it and how unfair it was that she had all this responsibility.

Then an interesting thing happened. One sister changed her mind and invited their father to come and live with her for awhile. She prepared his meals and took him to dialysis. She wasn't as interested in taking care of their father as she was in giving her sister a break. She cared for him for several months before returning him to Betty. In addition, when their father was in the hospital, which he frequently was, another sister either personally took her turn sitting with their father, or she hired an off-duty nurse to sit in her place. On more than one occasion, the sister who lived about 3,000 miles away would fly home and spend a week or so staying with their father while he was in the hospital.

No matter how many people helped Betty care for her father, nor how much anybody did, Betty clung to her anger and continued to play the role of victim, criticizing everything and everybody around her. It's now been more than a decade since Betty's father died, yet Betty continues to describe the experience of caring for her father as one that she endured totally alone, without any help from John, their daughters, her sisters, or anybody else. Betty is still angry and she holds much resentment towards her sisters. John told me that the process of caring for Betty's father could have been very different, and perhaps could have even been a pleasant experience, were it not for

Betty's attitude. John was quick to say that Betty's father was actually a pleasant man to be around, after he stopped drinking. The man was intelligent. He was well-read and contributed much to their conversations. John seemed sad that the experience had been so negative for Betty, yet he realized that it was only negative because Betty chose for it to be.

Here is another story that is probably somewhere in the middle of the spectrum. I will refer to these people as Pat and Karen. At the point when Pat's mother could no longer safely live by herself, Pat moved his mother in with him and his wife, Karen. Karen did not want Pat's mother to move in. She had never enjoyed a relationship with her mother-in-law and she surely did not want to be involved in taking care of her. Pat's mother had too many assets to qualify for Medicaid, yet she didn't have enough money to pay the private rate for care. So it seemed to Pat that he had no choice but to move his mother into his own home. He assured Karen that he would take care of his mother. He would do her laundry. He would take her to her medical appointments and whatever else she needed. He realized this was his responsibility. He did not expect Karen to help.

This went okay for a few months, then Karen became jealous that Pat was doing so much for his mother. Karen perceived that Pat was always involved with things surrounding his mother and he no longer had time for her. She resented this and started picking fights with him. Soon, Karen began setting up situations so Pat would have to choose between her and his mother. The tension and stress became almost too great for Pat to handle. He started getting sick more frequently. He told me he reached a point when he no longer enjoyed anything. He dreaded going home and he began drinking heavily, which only added to his conflict with Karen. This situation lasted for about five years and Karen filed for divorce. That was several years ago, and when I last talked with Pat, which now must have been about a year ago, his mother was still living with him. As you can imagine, Pat has many mixed emotions about this. He told me he takes it one day at a time. He has learned a lot about himself and his relationships and he has quit drinking. He said he is concerned about his own future, since he has no children of his own. He wonders who will take care of him when the time comes that he can no longer live alone.

> Karen began setting up situations so Pat would have to choose between her and his mother.

The last story I want to tell you is all the way at the other end of the spectrum. Remember, there are all sorts of stories in between. This particular story involved two close friends of mine. I will just call them Carol and Tom. Tom's mother had an irreversible lung disease and his stepfather was diabetic. His stepfather had no living relatives willing to assume the responsibility of taking care of him, so Tom's mother and stepfather came as a package. Even though Carol and Tom were both professionals, and it was Tom's relatives, the responsibility of taking care of them was delegated to Carol. It wasn't that Tom was unwilling to take care of his mother and stepfather, he simply felt inadequate as to how to go about it. Carol had maintained a loving relationship with Tom's folks for many years. Consequently, they trusted her to make decisions for them. They knew she would make decisions in their best interest.

Carol told me she felt overwhelmed. She described her experience as following this sequence: Tom's folks lived 2,000 miles away. As a result of diabetes, Tom's stepfather had his left leg amputated. Carol took time off from her job and flew to be with Tom's mother and stepfather during this period of time. She arranged home-healthcare workers to come and assist Tom's stepfather, starting the day he came home from the hospital. However, help did not arrive for several days. Since Tom's mother was not physically able to take care of her husband, Carol postponed her trip home so she could stay and help toilet, bathe and dress Tom's stepfather. Carol said this was embarrassing for all of them. She told me about one particular time when she had just finished helping Tom's father bathe and he told her, with tears in his eyes, how much he loved her and appreciated her taking care of them. Carol said she realized, at that moment, how pretentious modesty and ego really are. She said something else I will never forget; she said she had never felt so good about herself as a person. She realized she had no apparent obligation to this man, yet she knew there was an obligation that exceeded legal, marital, or family ties. That obligation was human-to-human. She said she understood, for the first time in her life, what it meant to be our brother's keeper.

> She said she understood, for the first time in her life, what it meant to be our brother's keeper.

Only a few months after Tom's stepfather had his leg amputated, it became obvious he and Tom's mother were in need of greater assistance. So Carol went and moved them to the city where she and Tom lived. Then, a few months later, it became necessary for Tom's mother and stepfather to move to an assisted living facility. Carol found a facility and, once again, handled everything. Moving them to a care facility was complicated by the fact that Tom's stepfather had been a successful attorney. Consequently, he had acquired many material possessions which included not one home, but three houses, located in different parts of the country. They had a primary residence back East; they had a winter home in Florida; they had a summer home in the mountains. Carol was the one to handle disposing of all these properties, and the furnishings, as well.

Not long after moving to the assisted living facility, Tom's mother had to take her husband to the doctor for a checkup. Since it was his left leg that had been amputated, Tom's stepfather could still drive. Consequently, they felt confident they could manage on their own, so they did not ask Tom or Carol to go with them. After the appointment, Tom's mother pushed her husband in his wheelchair to their car. Remember, this woman had an irreversible lung disease, so this was extremely taxing for her because her lungs were not operating at full capacity. Unfortunately, on the way home, Tom's mother could hardly catch her breath. She had a stroke in the car and had to be hospitalized. Then she became comatose and was placed on life-support. Carol said the decision to turn off the life-support machines was the most difficult decision they had ever had to make. Furthermore, she and Tom had never figured his mother would die before his stepfather.

Carol was honest to tell me she and Tom had, at some level, blamed his stepfather for her death. At another level, they knew he certainly was not responsible, but in their minds, if she had not been pushing him in the wheelchair, she wouldn't have exerted her lungs to that extent, and she might still be living. Carol was quick to say she and Tom also blamed themselves, and they felt very guilty.

Now, I want you to hear the *should* statement that underlies their guilt. Carol said she and Tom believed they *should* have known about the doctor's appointment, even though his mother had chosen not to tell them. And one of them *should* have gone with his parents to the doctor.

Shortly after his wife's death, Tom's stepfather declined to the level that he needed to be moved to a nursing home. So, once again, Carol found a home and moved him. Several months later, Tom's stepfather died. Carol told me that when she looked back on her experience of caring for Tom's mother and stepfather, she viewed it as the greatest learning experience of her life. She said she developed a capacity for tolerance and compassion she had never before experienced. Out of curiosity, I asked Carol how the responsibility to take care of Tom's mother and stepfather had been delegated to her. She said Tom was so overwhelmed that he was virtually paralyzed. Since there was no one else to take care of them, she felt she had to take over. Decisions had to be made and somebody had to take action.

> It seems some of us may, in fact, have more than one turn.

Carol became another statistic in the research which indicates the decision as to who will assume responsibility for elderly parents is often one of default, to women, even when it is their husband's parents. I also asked Carol, if she could change anything about this experience, what she would have done differently. She told me she would have spent more time with Tom's mother and stepfather. She ended by saying she was thankful for the opportunity to be the caregiver for Tom's mother and stepfather because she truly believed that experience prepared her for her upcoming role as caregiver for her own mother and father. It seems some of us may, in fact, have more than one turn.

You know, Kathryn, Dan Millman probably said it best in his marvelous book, The Sacred Journey of the Peaceful Warrior. He wrote, "I went to sleep and I dreamt that life was joy. I awoke to find that life was service and I lived to find that service was joy."

K: Thank you, Dr. Haymon. I see now there are so many different roles for the spouse of caregivers. What strikes me is that we truly do have a choice as to how we experience these very difficult times. Could you now walk us through how this all affects children and teenagers—even grandchildren?

S: While some caregivers still have adolescents and teenagers at home, many of us Baby Boomers are now in our 50's. Consequently, our children are grown and have children of their own. So the children we talk about might actually be the great-grandchildren of our parents. For the sake of example, I will simply refer to them as *your children*. Whether the elderly person is coming to live in your own home, or your children will just be visiting them, you need to take time to talk with them about the elderly person's condition. Although you will need to help the child understand the differences between problems associated with old age and problems associated with particular illnesses and impending death, you don't need to go into a lot of great detail with them. You only need to explain as much as the child can understand. Remember to keep it simple. When children understand that elderly people cannot help being the way they are, then it is easier for the child to tolerate certain behaviors and not take things personally.

> When children understand that elderly people cannot help being the way they are, then it is easier for the child to tolerate certain behaviors and not take things personally.

K: Could you give us some examples?

S: If the grandparents are frail and unable to walk as far or as fast as they once could, you might only need to tell the child that as we grow older our bones and muscles are not as strong as they once were. That is the reason they move so slowly.

K: What if the grandparents have dementia?

S: Then simply explain that, for whatever reason, the brain has become diseased and parts of the brain have been destroyed by the disease. Help the child to understand that sometimes information is destroyed or erased. That is why their grandparents cannot remember names or places or what they had for lunch. It is helpful to use analogies the child can understand. With younger children, you might liken this to an Etch-A-Sketch toy. Perhaps even allow them to draw something on it. Then erase it so they can see that the drawing that was once there is now gone. No matter how hard they shake that box, the drawing is not coming back. With older children, you might liken it to a computer, or maybe a calculator. Allow the child to input some numbers or type something. Then, without saving the information, turn the machine off and back on again. Help them understand that the machine did not forget the information just to be mean. Once the information is gone, the machine, like the diseased brain, just cannot get it back.

It is also useful to help the child understand that elderly people do not pick up things and misplace them to be mean or to aggravate them. They just cannot help it. Explain to them that many elderly people may pick up something and, by the time they turn around, they have forgotten what they were going to do with it, or where they got it in the first place. You might encourage children to put certain things that they don't want anybody touching in a special place that is not obvious to the elderly person. Try to anticipate what behaviors your children will view as strange and talk with them about those. It may be that their grandparents can no longer toilet themselves and need to wear diapers. Perhaps they have had a stroke and they have difficulty talking or moving an arm or a leg. No matter what the disability, talk to your children and allow them to talk to you about it. I know I have said in every section that we have to talk about these issues, but we have to talk about these issues!

> Another thing is, we need to give our children psychological permission to say whatever they want to say and feel whatever they need to feel.

Another thing is, we need to give our children psychological permission to say whatever they want to say and feel whatever they need to feel. Don't add guilt by telling them they *should* or *should not* feel a certain way. It is common for children to feel frightened of their grandparents, especially if the grandparent no longer talks or walks or looks the way she or he used to. Sometimes children are even afraid to touch them, so they don't want to hug them. It is important here to allow children to set their own boundaries. You may also need to reassure them that old age is not contagious. Sometimes children don't want to hug their grandparents or great-grandparents because they are afraid they will catch something.

K: That's interesting. I never thought of that.

S: Children also need to know they cannot make their grandparents worse. Explain to them that sometimes things they do might, in fact, upset their grandparents temporarily. However, their grandparents will probably forget the incident very quickly. At any rate, they will not make their grandparents sicker. Children are often afraid their grandparents will die. Since that is a real probability, don't be afraid to talk with them about death. Allow them to ask questions and talk about what death means to them. Explore how they feel, rather than tell them how they *ought* to feel. Don't just assume that children are not bothered by their grandparents' condition. Observe them as they interact with their grandparents, then find some quiet time and let them talk about their feelings. By all means, do not try to force children to participate in activities they are uncomfortable with. This is a difficult time for all of you, and every person copes with stress differently.

K: What are some of the most frequent things that come up for children?

S: Oh, when talking about their grandparents they say such things as: They smell funny; they have no teeth; the way they eat is sickening; they act crazy. I'm afraid of them; they're always touching me and messing with my hair; I have no privacy with them around; they are always coming into my room and bothering my things; they are hard of hearing so we have to scream at them and we have to play the TV so loud it hurts my ears; we can never go anywhere anymore because Grandmother or Grandfather can't walk that far or sit that long.

Teenagers commonly report such complaints as: I never have any time with my friends anymore because I have to watch out for them; I can't have my friends over because it upsets Grandma or Grandpa; I'm embarrassed to bring my friends over because of the way Grandma or Grandpa acts or looks; they are always telling me what to do; we don't have enough money to do the things we need to because we are always spending it on them; it's not fair that I have to give up my room for people I hardly even know.

> This complaint reinforces the notion that our family members would much rather have a rested, happy person than home-cooked meals.

Another common complaint about the caregiver is, "You're always tired and in a bad mood, now that you have to take care of Grandma, and you take it out on me." This complaint reinforces the notion that our family members would much rather have a rested, happy person than home-cooked meals. Even though it's important to observe your children, and explore things they appear to be concerned about, be careful that you don't make something an issue for them, just because it's an issue for you. Children experience the same emotions we do. The only difference may be in the way children express their emotions.

K: How do they express them?

S: It is common for children to act out when they are scared, unsure, or confused. Often, this acting out manifests in overt, aggressive behaviors like talking back, being disrespectful, challenging family rules, being especially mean to a younger brother or sister, or perhaps getting in trouble at school. Some children act out in passive-aggressive ways, like conveniently forgetting to do chores or deliver messages, or perhaps by breaking something or throwing something away by accident. Some children just close down all together and they will not talk at home. No matter how many times you ask them what's wrong, they just shrug and say, "Nothing." It is very common for children of divorced parents to decide they want to live with the other parent when things change drastically in their own home. I certainly cannot tell you how to handle each and every circumstance. You know your children and your family situation much better than anyone else. However, I want to stress the need to keep communication lines open. We need to talk and talk and talk, then talk some more, about all of the issues surrounding taking care of an elderly loved one.

K: You have said before that it can be a positive experience for an adult. Is there a way to make it a positive experience for a child?

S: I believe children need to be given opportunities to do things for elderly relatives. Ask your children what they think they could do to help out, or something they would like to do for their grandparents. Although I hated my assigned job of emptying my grandmother's bed pan, I enjoyed picking and bringing flowers to her because that was my idea. That was what I wanted to do. I also enjoyed drawing and coloring pictures for her. She always seemed pleased and would brag on what a good job I had done. It also seems comforting for us to have memories of things we have done for others to recall, after they are no longer with us. I think this is also true for children. We need to convey to children the positive things we all have to gain from elderly individuals.

K: What would be some examples of that?

S: You might suggest to your children that they get their grandparents to tell them about the times when they were growing up. If you don't already have one, buy an inexpensive tape recorder so your children can tape their conversations with their grandparents. This may be a source of comfort in the future, not only for the children, but for other family members as well. You might also encourage your children to take photos of their grandparents and start a book of memories. Helping your children get to know their grandparents happens naturally in most families, just by spending time together. However, if the elderly relatives live in another state, or maybe they are in a care facility and visits are limited, children can be helped to engage with them by thinking of things they could talk about, prior to their visits. Younger children may feel comforted by asking specific, yet fanciful, questions about favorite songs, favorite books, or favorite colors.

> You might suggest to your children that they get their grandparents to tell them about the times when they were growing up.

They may ask their grandparents how they picked their mom's or dad's name. Who was their favorite president and why? Who was their hero? Or, if you could change one thing in the world, what would you change? I would encourage children to come up with their own questions and write them down or record them. Kathryn, it's especially useful to watch how the elderly person responds when she or he looks back over eighty or ninety years. It is interesting to note their response when you ask them, if they could change one thing, what would they change? By involving children, we give them an opportunity to see we all have so much to learn from elderly people. Adolescents and teenagers are an entirely different topic.

K: In more ways than one.

S: Usually, they feel more comfortable participating in adult conversations. Even when that happens though, don't expect them to lead the conversation or even to be particularly responsive. Just being there is enough. There may be many things elderly people are still able to do and they might enjoy teaching their grandchildren or great-grandchildren these things. Carl's mother taught me a lot about cooking, embroidering, and fishing. She also taught me how to dig for worms so that we would have fish bait. The important thing here is to recognize that each child will have her or his own relationship with her or his grandparents. So encourage your children to participate in the caregiving process as much as they want to, yet respect whatever feelings they have.

> By involving children, we give them an opportunity to see we all have so much to learn from elderly people.

K: Dr. Haymon, thank for sharing so much of your personal life with us, and for doing the research. We hope, and I know you hope, that this will save a lot of time and energy for the millions of Americans and their families who will be experiencing their turn sooner than they possibly think. Again, thank you.

CHAPTER 8

DEATH AND GRIEF

K: Dr. Haymon, we've talked about the emotional issues for the caregiver, the elderly person, and for family members. Inevitably, the time comes when our elderly loved ones die. Please talk to us about this final phase of the caregiving process.

S: In order for us to understand where we are in any process, it is often helpful to start with a historical perspective. As I mentioned earlier, when we look back to the period in time when the majority of people in our country farmed, and there were two or three generations that lived on the same farm, maybe even in the same house, families were expected to take care of their elderly. That was part of life. And because there were usually lots of family members to help out, it didn't seem such a burden. Being old and dependent was as much a part of life as being young and dependent. Illness and poor health for the elderly were viewed as being as natural as strength and vitality for the young. There was no denial about death. There was respect for life, because death was understood as part of the process of living. People died at home, with dignity. Their family and friends surrounded them to support them in the next step of their eternal journey. It was even common for family and friends to prepare the body for burial. The body then remained at home for two or three days so loved ones and friends could come by and pay their last respects. For the most part, work stopped for those few days. Family and friends gathered and, in their own ways, celebrated the person's life and the parts of it they'd shared. Often they sat in the room with the casket and told one story after another. It seemed to me that the person's spirit remained and shared in the closure taking place. I experienced this when my own grandparents died when I was little. As I look back on those memories, I see the benefits of that process.

K: What do you remember?

S: When I was a little girl, probably three or four years old, my great-uncle died. I remember sitting in the front room of my grandmother's home. The casket was in that room and lots of family members sat around. Relatives told stories and laughed. During that period in time, it was common for families to sit up all night with the deceased person. They sort of took shifts. A few family members would sit with the body for awhile, then they might leave and take a break while other family members would come to sit. People just kind of wandered in and out, but there was always somebody there to support the person on this next step of her or his spiritual journey. It was like we were all there supporting him in death. It reminds me of something the Aborigines say: When a baby is born, every tribe member comes by and says, "We're happy you're here and we support you in your journey." Then, when someone dies, everyone in the tribe comes by and says, "We support you in your journey."

It seems to me, it was sort of like that. I didn't really know my great-uncle because I had only seen him three or four times in my life and I was quite young. What I do remember are the stories. What immortalized him in my mind was not what I actually remembered about my own interactions with him, but what I remembered from the great stories other relatives told. There were lots of wonderful and funny stories, things about his kindness and his sense of humor. Then one of my great-aunts said she remembered when she got into this squabble with him and she relived the event as though it had been the day before. What that did for me was to normalize his life and help me realize there is good and bad in everyone. For every person who would change us, there's someone who loves us just the way we are. It also seems to me, as unique as we truly are, we're really not very different from one another.

> For every person who would change us, there's someone who loves us just the way we are.

K: You said your mother actually held you up to kiss your grandfather goodbye.

S: I was a little over four when my mother's father died. My mom had told me, "If you kiss a dead person 'bye, then you won't have any nightmares or any bad dreams about them." So she held me up and I leaned over the casket. I looked at my grandpa and, when I leaned over to kiss him on the cheek, my mom said, "Be sure you don't kiss him too hard because you will bruise him." So, very gently, I leaned over and kissed my grandpa 'bye, and his cheek was very, very cold. I remember pulling back a little and thinking that was strange. Then I just lightly kissed him again.

K: But you weren't frightened by that?

S: Oh no, I wasn't frightened at all. His cold face just seemed a little strange to me. I remember, a year or so ago, when my little cousin was at a funeral. It was the child's great-grandfather, and a very similar thing happened. I was so happy to watch as his mother held him up to kiss his grandpa 'bye. He kissed his grandpa and said, "Oh Grandpa's cold. I'll get him a blanket." That scene brought back very positive memories for me. There was a lot of closure in my experience. I was able to kiss my grandpa and say goodbye. It was all very positive. I'm so thankful for the stories my other relatives shared. If not for their stories, I wouldn't remember some of my relatives at all.

K: From a psychological standpoint, does it help for people to participate in the dying process of others?

S: It may help us come to some realization about our own mortality. For many, those moments of quiet introspection remind them, in the end, that relationships may be all that really matter. I remember those who died while struggling in relationships of disharmony, needing others to be wrong so they could be right. There was tremendous sadness. There seemed to be a cloud of heaviness in the realization they had died without resolving their own internal struggles. They lacked self-acceptance. It now seems to me that the only ones who feared death were those who were dissatisfied with their lives. For others, who resolved their internal conflicts as they moved along life's path, there seemed to be a peace about their death reflected in others. There was appropriate sadness without hysteria, and a joyfulness in the privilege of having known them.

K: So, Dr. Haymon, you're really advocating that the entire family —from the youngest to the oldest— get involved in the final process.

S: Yes, I am. It seems taking part in a loved one's dying process provides an opportunity for us to work through lots of tender emotions. However, as history was being written, we moved from a rural way of life into what would become known as the Industrial Revolution. For those who did not have transportation, it became necessary to live near the towns and the factories. Many of the older people refused to leave their farms, so families separated. Physical distance created emotional distance.

By staying pre-occupied with other things, some could postpone emotional pain.

Life during the Industrial Period continued to accelerate. Soon, there was hardly time for death, much less the dying process. Many people died without their loved ones there to support them. Relatives and friends were usually notified by phone or telegram or letter. They weren't there with them. Families were hardly inconvenienced at all. This was the first generation in our history to delegate responsibilities associated with the death of loved ones to total strangers. Funeral homes would take care of everything. Families could spend a couple of hours receiving guests and friends at the chapel, which was conveniently located in the same building where the body was prepared for burial. Paying last respects would be done in the evening. The funeral could be scheduled for the following afternoon so people wouldn't have to miss any more work than necessary. Close friends and family could come by the designated house right after the funeral; everyone could still be home to catch the ten o'clock news, then back to work the following morning. If people moved really fast, they could deny death had occurred at all.

Weeks later, some would think about dropping by the nursing home for a visit. Then some faint part of their memory would remind them their loved one had died. They would vaguely recall the funeral and scratch their heads in confusion as to how it had all happened so fast, as though it had been a dream. Feelings of emptiness would be attributed to their sense of loss. They'd convince themselves that what they really needed to do was to stay busy so they wouldn't have to think about it. Many would do exactly that. By staying preoccupied with other things, some could postpone emotional pain. They could forfeit the occasion to celebrate the person's life, or to even assess their own, and abort any chance of closure.

It seems to me, we've lost something in this evolutionary process. The last several funerals I've gone to, I've seen no children, and I knew the people had grandchildren. Some even had great-grandchildren. I wondered how these children were being taught to say goodbye and bring closure to relationships. Whenever I ask the parents where the children are, I'm told things like, "Well, I didn't see any need in taking them out of school," or, "I was afraid they would make too much noise," or, "I didn't want to upset them." There is great therapeutic value in children taking part in rituals and ceremonies, and being allowed to *feel*.

> Too many times, they deny a relationship was important to them because it was negative or unresolved or filled with anger and resentment.

It's natural to be upset and sad when someone dies. How will they learn to deal with their emotions, if they're not allowed to feel them? It also seemed to me that some of the adults were robotically going through the motions of the burial ceremony, not even allowing themselves to feel. Many times, I see clients who come for counseling because they're depressed. I often learn they have never grieved the losses of significant relationships. Too many times, they deny a relationship was important to them because it was negative or unresolved or filled with anger and resentment. Some people pretend only positive relationships are meaningful.

K: That's interesting.

S: The irony may be that relationships which have unresolved anger and resentment are the very ones we have the most to gain from. If our relationships with others are, in fact, mirrored reflections of our relationship with ourselves, then we have at least as much to learn about ourselves from our so-called negative relationships, as those we refer to as positive.

K: But how can we resolve issues with someone who has already passed away?

S: When my biological father died, I was still angry with him. Enraged would be a better word. Not only had he been alcoholic, but he was criminally abusive to me and my sisters and I guess to my brother. I don't know whether my brother was abused. I don't remember much about him because he left home and joined the Navy when I was just three years old. Besides being abusive to me and my sisters, my father was also abusive to my mother. There were many times when I feared for our lives. As a child, I hated him, and I used to pray he would die, just so the abuse would stop. But he didn't die until I was about 30 years old. Even though I didn't see him much those last few years, I still harbored much anger and resentment, and I guess maybe even hatred for him. So, the few days between the time he died and the time he was buried, I didn't know what to do with my anger. While I was processing my feelings, trying to sort all this out, I recognized that my worst fear had been realized. Remember when we talked about anger being one layer up from fear?

K: Yes.

S: While I was processing my feelings, I looked under my anger and saw my fear. My worst fear was that he would die before things changed, and I would never have the father I wanted. That had happened! When I looked around, I also realized I had lived through it. I had lived through my worst fear; he was gone. I was so sad. I sat down and wrote him a letter. I told him how much I had always wanted a good relationship with him, how much I had wanted us to be a happy family, and how sad I was we'd never been able to. I told him in the letter that I hoped, somewhere in time and space, we would be given the opportunity to have the love and happiness we had not had here. I told him how sorry I was he had been in so much emotional pain that he'd had to use alcohol to anesthetize himself. Then I noticed my anger was gone. I had forgiven him. I felt so light I wasn't even sure I was touching the ground. Then I felt something that felt very strange at first, and I wasn't sure what it was. So I sat there very quietly, just allowing myself to feel whatever this was. Then the strangest notion came to me. Underneath all that, I loved him. He'd had a horrible childhood himself, and just didn't know how to let go of his own anger and resentment, so he took it out on us. I told him in the letter how much I loved him and I hoped one day I'd be given the opportunity to show him that love. I also told him I hoped he would now be in peace and out of his pain. I took the letter to the funeral home and I placed it inside his coat pocket, right over his heart. Then I kissed him and said goodbye.

> My worst fear was that he would die before things changed, and I would never have the father I wanted.

K: Dr. Haymon, thank you for sharing that story with us. I know it was not easy, and I hope others will benefit from your willingness to share it. What about a situation where we still have unresolved anger and resentment with a relative and they died many years ago? Can we still come to this kind of letting go, many, many years past their death?

S: Writing a letter to someone you have unresolved issues with, or you haven't brought closure to, is a very old technique. It is also very effective. Even if the person's been gone for years, go ahead and write the letter. Say all the things you wish you had said while she or he was living, or maybe that you need to say now. Vent whatever anger and frustration you might have, then try to look underneath the anger for the fear. You may have to look very closely, but it's there. When you see your fear, look around and know you have lived through it. Sometimes, emotional pain is so great we're afraid, if we acknowledge it, we might not live through it. When you realize you have in fact lived through perhaps your worst fear, your worst nightmare, and you're still alive, close your eyes and feel the peacefulness that comes with that realization. In my case, I felt so light I wasn't sure I was still sitting in the chair. I felt so light because the anger and fear were gone. It truly is amazing to me, even as a psychologist, when I look at this phenomenon. People come to my office and they're so burdened — heavy with anger and fear. Then, weeks or maybe months later, when they've worked through some of their anger and fear, when they've let go of it, they physically look lighter. They physically look lighter. For me, it was a wonderful feeling. You'll know when your anger is gone and your fear is gone because you will feel lighter. So take a couple of deep breaths and enjoy it. It feels wonderful. Then write whatever you feel in your letter. If you need to say you forgive them, then do so. Remember, you've already written "I'm still angry," or "I hate your guts," or whatever. Once you've looked past all that, your anger and your fear, write whatever else you feel. If you need to say, "I forgive you," "I love you," "I feel compassion for you," "I feel sorry for you," whatever you need to say, write it in your letter. Put everything you feel in the letter. Then put it in an envelope, address it to that person, Somewhere in the Universe. Don't put a return address on it, but put a stamp on it and go mail it.

> We can't let go of the anger until we see what's driving it, and the driving force is fear.

K: Do you have to really go through this process of actually mailing the letter? Can't you just do that and then tear it up and throw it in the waste basket? Wouldn't it have the same effect?

S: Absolutely mail it. How much is a stamp? Thirty-two cents and another nickel for an envelope? Put it in an envelope and address it to John Doe, Somewhere in the Universe, and mail it.

K: It's cheaper than an hour with a psychologist. Let me ask you this: Could you do it with someone who's living, or do you have to do this with someone who has passed away?

S: I think it's just as important to write letters from your heart to people who are still living. It's almost a dress rehearsal with a chance to say what you really want to say. Sometimes, we psychologists use what is called " the empty-chair technique." You pretend the person you want to talk to is in the chair, and you actually curse them out, or say to them whatever you need to say. But letter writing is something you can do just for you. Nobody else is listening. You can write down everything you want to say to that person. Get out all of the anger, the frustration, and the resentment. But the important thing here is that we really must look under the anger in order to see the fear. We can't let go of the anger until we see what's driving it, and the driving force is fear. So we look at the fear, then we look around and realize we lived through it. Remember, sometimes people don't want to face emotional pain because they're afraid they won't live through it. Emotional pain is just as real as physical pain.

K: But if they're living, do you still send it to them, or do you maybe think about it before you send it?

S: Oh, you just do the same thing. You put their name on it, address it to them, Somewhere in the Universe, and mail it.

K: Okay. That's what I'm looking for. In other words, don't really mail it to them?

S: I wouldn't mail it to them first. I would go ahead and mail it to them Somewhere in the Universe, then see how you feel over the next several days and just kind of process that. There may come a time when you really do want to talk to the person.

K: I'll share a personal note someone once told me. In fact, it was quite recently. They said to write down feelings I have for my mother, which I have trouble verbalizing, before she dies, not after she dies. They're very positive feelings; I just never said them. I came home after I heard this and wrote her a letter and told her what she really meant to me. I really looked for things that made her special to me and it was wonderful. I sent it to her and she loved it! I think she carries it with her now, and I'm so glad I did that. So, in both senses, I can see where the letter writing technique could be really valuable for those who are listening today.

> ...it is just as important to tell people all of the wonderful things you've never said, but wished you had.

S: It is very valuable and I'm glad you brought that up, because it is just as important to tell people all of the wonderful things you've never said, but wished you had. Or maybe you just want to remind them of how you feel. Maybe you have told them, "I love you," a thousand, million times, and you just want to tell them again. In that case, put their real address on it.

K: Thank you, Dr. Haymon, that was interesting.

S: I would like to talk about one last thing—the value of staying in touch with your own internal feelings. Sometimes, even in the face of much information to the contrary, our own heartfelt feelings tell us to do just the opposite of what our brain is telling us to do. I encourage people to pay attention to those feelings. All too often, we're inundated with so much information that we seem paralyzed as to what to do. Then, unfortunately, we start looking outside ourselves for answers, and maybe even for somebody else to make our decisions for us. One of the ways I identify when I'm in this position is to note my confusion. Sometimes I think, oh well, maybe I'll go to the left or maybe I'll go to the right; maybe I'll go forward; maybe I'll back up; I don't really know what I'm doing. Perhaps you've heard the old saying, "You just stand there turning around in circles because you don't know which way to go."

K: Now wait a minute, I thought you had all the answers. We're in big trouble here if you're going in right, reverse, and forward.

S: Well, I do feel that sometimes, and when I do, it's helpful for me to find a place where I can be still, where I can be quiet. Then I listen to my own inner

> You may choose to experience this process as difficult, stressful and unpleasant. You may also choose to experience it as positive, meaningful and as adding value to your life. It is your choice.

voice. I block out all the chatter from outside and look within. We all have this wonderful gift of being inner-directed. It's an internal mechanism that really will guide us, if we'll just take the time to pay attention to it. That's when we make decisions that are in our highest good, and if it's in our highest good, it's also in the highest good of everything in the universe. So trust yourself. When you feel torn between what you *feel* and what you *think*, take a moment to get in touch with what you feel, then trust that feeling. It doesn't matter that everything outside of you is screaming the opposite. If you really have taken the time to get in touch with your feelings, then go with the feeling. Caring for an aging loved one can be a wonderful opportunity for you to learn more about yourself, to learn more about them, to learn more about humanity in general. The entire process is absolutely neutral. You may choose to experience this process as difficult, stressful and unpleasant. You may also choose to experience it as positive, meaningful, and as adding value to your life. It is your choice.

When I look back on these past few years, as I've taken care of my mother and stepfather, I think about Charles Dickens and what he wrote in <u>A Tale of Two Cities</u>, "It was the best of times, it was the worst of times…" Having the opportunity to provide care for them has truly been, and continues to be, a rewarding, learning experience in my own growth process. It's enabled me to examine my own values, as well as come to terms with my own mortality. My emotions have run the full gamut. My heart goes out to each and every one of you. And I sincerely wish you the very best as you take your turn.

* * * * * * * * *

For further information or additional materials, contact Dr. Sandra Haymon at Magnolia Productions, P.O. Box 13705, Tallahassee, Florida 32317-3705.

RESOURCES

The following addresses and phone numbers are subject to change. All efforts were made to ensure accuracy at the time of this publication.

ABUSE

National Center on Elder Abuse
1-202-682-2470: 810 First St. NE, Suite 500, Washington, DC 20002-4257
Free information and state referrals to protective agencies

ADULT DAY CARE SERVICES

National Adult Day Services Association
1-202-479-1200: c/o National Council on the Aging, Inc.(NCOA),
409 3rd St. SW, Suite 200, Washington, DC 20024
Provides free publications: Your Guide to Selecting an Adult Day Center;
Adult Day Care Fact Sheet; Why Adult Day Care; and
National Council on the Aging (NCOA) Resources Catalogue

Nursing Home Information Service—National Council of Senior Citizens
1-202-347-8800 (ext 340/341): 1331 F Street NW, Washington, DC 20004
Provides information on adult day-care, long-term care, home-healthcare, and care communities

AFRO-AMERICAN ELDER SERVICES

National Caucus and Center on Black Aged
1-202-637-8400: 1424 K St. NW, Suite 500, Washington, DC 20005
Provides local referrals

ALASKAN NATIVES ELDER SERVICES

National Indian Council on Aging
1-505-888-3302: 6400 Uptown Blvd. NE City Center, Suite 510W,
Albuquerque, NM 87110
Provides information and nationwide referrals for Alaskan natives and American Indians

ALCOHOL AND SUBSTANCE ABUSE

Alcoholics Anonymous
1-212-870-3400: P.O. Box 459 Grand Central Station, New York, NY 10163
Provides nationwide referrals to local chapters

AL-Anon Family Groups
1-800-356-9996: P.O. Box 862, Midtown Station, New York, NY10018
Provides nationwide referrals to local chapters, and brochures

National Clearinghouse for Alcohol and Drug Information
1-800-729-6686: P.O. Box 2345, Rockville, MD 20847
Provides publications on prevention and treatment

National Council on Alcoholism and Drug Dependence
1-800-622-2255: 12 West 21st St., New York, NY 10010
Provides nationwide referrals to local chapters, and free information

AMERICAN INDIAN ELDER SERVICES

National Association of Area Agencies on Aging
1-800-677-1116: 1112 16th Street NW, Suite 100, Washington, DC 20036
Provides information and representation to 190 Native American organizations of federally-recognized tribes

National Indian Council on Aging
1-505-888-3302: 6400 Uptown Blvd. NE, City Center, Ste 510W, Albuquerque, NM 87110
Provides information and nationwide referrals for American Indians and Alaskan natives

ASIAN/PACIFIC ELDER SERVICES

National Pacific/Asian Resource Center on Aging
1-206-624-1221: Melbourne Tower, 1511 Third Ave., Suite 914, Seattle, WA 98101
Provides information, publications and direct services for Asian and Pacific elderly

CAREGIVERS, SERVICES FOR AND CARE MANAGERS

AARP—American Association of Retired Persons
1-800-424-3410: 601 East St. NW, Washington, DC 20049

Membership includes: 24-hour hotline; subscription to bulletin; discounts on hotels/motels, and rental cars; insurance benefits (car, life, homeowners); pharmacy services; investment and credit card programs; legal counsel; online computer services provided through America On-line, Prodigy and CompuServe. Membership fees: 1 year-$8.00; 3 years-$20.00; 10 years-$45.00. Members must be 50 years of age or older

Adult Help USA
1-800-422-4453

Provides crisis counseling, information and referrals, all counselors have at least a master's degree and specialized training in abuse and neglect issues. This is a Clearinghouse/National Network of Information for Abuse, Neglect or Exploitation of Elders

Aging Network Services
1-301-657-4329: 4400 East West Highway, Suite 907, Bethesda, MD 20814
Provides fee-for-service referrals to local care managers. Helpful to scattered families

American Self-Help Clearinghouse
1-201-625-7101: St. Clare's Riverside Medical Center, 25 Pocono Rd.,
Denville, NJ 07834
Provides local referrals to support groups

American Society on Aging
1-415-974-9600: 833 Market Street, San Francisco, CA 74103
Provides publications regarding caregiving of the aged

Caregivers Program
1-612-642-2055: A.H. Wilder Foundation, 919 Lafond Ave., St. Paul, MN 55104
Provides publications regarding care of the caregiver

CAPS — Children of Aging Parents
1-215-945-6900: Woodbourne Office Campus, 1609 Woodbourne Road,
Levittown, PA 19057
Provides local referrals and information on caregiver issues, support groups, and care managers

DISABILITIES and HANDICAPS

Access Foundation
1-516-568-2715: 1109 Linden Street, Valley Stream, NY 11580

Provides Internet clearinghouse information ($5.00 per search or $45.00 per year membership fee includes unlimited searches); and local referrals for information, services, equipment

Adaptive Environments Center
1-617-695-1225: 374 Congress Street, Suite 301, Boston, MA 02210

Provides training, information and publications including: A Consumer's Guide to Home Adaptation, $12.00. A non-profit organization

American Association of Retired Persons
1-800-424-3410: 601 E Street NW, Washington, DC 20049

Provides consumer information; technical design information for contractors; and publications including: The Do-Able, Renewable Home, and A Perfect Fit. A membership organization

Center for Universal Design
1-800-647-6777: North Carolina University, P.O. Box 8613, Raleigh, NC 27695

Provides information and publications on home modifications and accessible housing

Direct Link for the Disabled Hotline
1-805-688-1603

Provides information from 12,000 local organizations that offer services for the disabled

National Rehabilitation Information Center and ABLEDATA
1-800-346-2742 or 1-800-227-0216 or Internet naric@capaccess.org

8455 Colesville Rd., Suite 935, Silver Springs, MD 20910

Provides database information on equipment and home modification; and referrals to local rehabilitation centers and organizations which provide help for the disabled. A federally-funded, for fee organization

Paralyzed Veterans of America
1-800-424-8200: 801 18th Street NW, Washington, DC 20420

Provides information on benefits, home modifications, and adjusting to and living with a disability; and local referrals

DRIVING

Department of Highway Safety
Consult your local telephone directory

Provides a medical review board; suspension or revocation of driver's license; and addresses issues involving safe driving

AAA Foundation for Traffic Safety
1-800-305-7233 or 1-202-638-5944: 1440 New York Ave. NW, Suite 201, Washington, DC 20005

Provides information; publications; videos; a self-exam and training program for elderly individuals

National Safety Council
1-800-621-7619 or 1-800-621-6244 or 1-312-527-4800: 1121 Spring Lake Dr., Itasca, IL 60143

Provides free information; local referrals and a course for elderly drivers called "Coaching the Mature Driver."

FINANCIAL

American Institute of Certified Public Accountants
1-800-862-4270: 1211 Ave. of the Americas, New York, NY 100036
Provides information on estate and financial planning; and local referrals.
A professional organization

American Safe Deposit Association
1-317-888-1118: 330 West Main Street, Greenwood, IN 46142
Provides help in determining if a deceased person had a safe deposit box

American Society of Chartered Life Underwriters and Chartered Financial Consultants
1-800-392-6900: 270 South Bryn Mawr Ave., Bryn Mawr, PA 19010
Provides information and local referrals

Certified Financial Planners
1-303-830-7543: Board of Standards, 1660 Lincoln St., Suite 3050, Denver, CO 80264
Provides information regarding Certified Financial Planners current standing; and provisions for filing complaints

EHR—Elderly Homeowner Rehabilitation Program
Consult your local phone book
Provides grants for making deferred loans for home rehabilitation: State Health and Rehabilitative Services (HRS) may offer this assistance

Home Energy Assistance Program
Local agencies may offer this assistance
Assists elderly persons whose utilities have been disconnected, or are in danger of being disconnected. Local elder care agencies may advise you which agencies have been awarded these funds

Home Ownership Subsidy Program
Consult your local Dept. of Housing and Urban Development (HUD)
Assists low-income elderly persons in purchasing a home

Institute of Certified Financial Planners
1-800-282-7526 or 1-303-751-7600:
7600 E. Eastman Ave., Suite 301, Denver, CO 80231-4397
Provides a list of certified financial planners according to zip code, and free publication Selecting a Qualified Financial Planning Professional: Twelve Questions to Consider, and local referrals

International Association for Financial Planning
1-800-945-IAFP or 1-800-945-4237:
5775 Glenridge Dr. NE, Suite B-300, Atlanta, GA 30328-5364
Provides a local list of qualified planners, and a free publication: Consumer Guide to Comprehensive Financial Planning. A trade association

Internal Revenue Service
1-800-829-1040 for tax information: 1-800-829-3676 to order free publications and tax forms

IRAs—Individual Retirement Accounts (tax deferred personal savings)
Contact your banker or other financial consultant

National Association of Personal Financial Advisors
1-800-366-2732 or 1-708-557-7722:
1130 West Lake Cook Rd., Suite 150, Buffalo Grove, IL 60089
Provides information and local referrals for fee-only planners

National Association of Securities Dealers
1-800-289-9999: 9513 Key West Ave., Rockville, MD 20850
Provides information regarding complaints filed against brokerage firms or individual brokers

(Reverse Mortgages)
Works similarly to normal mortgages, only in reverse; allows senior citizens to receive monthly income while remaining in their homes.
Contact your local bank, or other lending institutions, or contact:

Federal National Mortgage Association (FNMA/Fannie Mae)
1-800-732-6643:
Public Information Office, 3900 Wisconsin Ave. NW, Washington, DC 20016
Provides free information regarding reverse mortgages

National Center for Home Equity Conversion
1-800-247-6553 or 1-612-953-4474:
7373 147th St. West, Suite 115, Apple Valley, MN 55124
Provides information and a publication:Your New Retirement Nest Egg, for $24.95

National Endowment for Financial Education
1-303-220-1200: 4695 S. Monaco St., Denver, CO 80237-3403
Provides information regarding planning your financial future and a free publication: Wealth Care Kit

National Foundation for Consumer Credit
1-800-388-2227: 8611 Second Ave., Suite 100, Silver Springs, MD 20910
Provides local referrals

Pension Rights Center
1-202-296-3776: 918 16th St. NW, Suite 704, Washington, DC 20006
Provides information and guidance

Section Eight Housing or Rental Assistance Program
Consult your local Dept. of Housing and Urban Development (HUD)
Supplements rental payments

Securities Exchange Commission
1-202-942-8088: 450 Fifth St. NW, Washington, DC 20549
Provides background information regarding financial planners; and complaints filed against financial planners

Social Security Administration
1-800-772-1213
Provides information regarding social security benefits, and direct deposit

FRAUD

Fraud Hotline
1-800-447-8477: HHS Tips Fraud Hotline, P.O. Box 23489, Washington, DC 20026
Hotline for reporting crime from health service workers or programs

Fraud of Social Security Issues
1-800-269-0271

Medicare Hotline
1-800-638-6833 or 1-800-492-6603 (Maryland)
Provides free information; answers questions; reports Medicare fraud

Ombudsman Council
Consult your local phone book under State Agencies
Handles complaints pertaining to nursing homes and other long-term care facilities

GENERAL INFORMATION

American Red Cross
1-202-737-8300: 430 17th Street NW, Washington, DC 20006, or
Consult your local telephone directory
Provides local referrals for training of elder caregiving

Catholic Charities USA
1-703-549-1390: 1731 King St., Alexandria, VA 22314
Provides local referrals

Choice in Dying
1-800-989-WILL or 1-212-366-5540: 200 Varick St., New York, NY 10014-0148
Provides state specific living wills and durable power of attorney

Community Resources
Consult your local place of worship (churches, synagogues, temples, etc.)
Provides a wide array of services

Consumer Information Center
1-719-948-3334: "Catalogue," Pueblo, CO 81009
Provides over 200 free consumer publications. This is a federal agency

Elder Helpline
1-800-262-2243
Provides referrals to local agencies, and general information

Eldercare Locator
1-800-677-1116
Provides information and local referrals that offer help with elder care needs

Elder Support Network
1-800-634-7346: Services of the Association of Jewish Family and Children's Agencies, P.O. Box 248, Kendall Park, NJ 08824-0248
Provides local referrals

FEMA—Federal Emergency Management Agency
1-800-462-9029:
FEMA National Tele-registration Center, P.O. Box 2312, Denton, TX 76202-2312
Provides disaster relief only when the President declares your area a national disaster through an act of nature. If your area is not declared a national disaster: Contact your county or state emergency management officials (local police departments may provide you with phone numbers and contact persons)

Food Stamp Program
Consult your local telephone directory or call Social Security at 1-800-772-1213
Provides supplemental income for nutritional needs. State HRS may offer this assistance

Hemlock Society USA
1-800-247-7421: P.O. Box 101810, Denver, CO 80250
Provides information and support of euthanasia (refusal of life-sustaining treatment and/or physician assisted suicide); publications; telephone counseling; and local referrals

Kelly Assisted Living
1-800-937-5355 or consult your local telephone directory:

Provides information packages on local service providers; in-home companionship and care to individuals who need assistance with daily living activities for short- and long-term disabilities (surgery recovery, Alzheimer's, etc.)

Local Elder Care Services
Contact your local elder care agency

May provide adult day care; respite relief and care services; companion services; telephone reassurance; home maintenance; lawn care; house cleaning; grocery shopping assistance; transportation; Adopt-A-Grandparent Program; Senior Work Program; Foster Grandparent Program

New Ways to Work
1-415-995-9860: 785 Market St., Suite 950, San Francisco, CA 94103

Provides information regarding work restructuring for caregivers

New York State Partnership for Long-term Care
1-518-473-7705: NYS DSS, 40 N. Pearl St., Albany, NY 12243

Provides information regarding Medicaid and private insurance companies offering long-term care policies and asset protection. New York residents only

Older Americans Act
Consult your local elder care agency—available in all communities

Subsidizes state community assisted living programs; Meals-On-Wheels; congregate meal sites

Senior Citizens Centers
Contact your local Senior Citizens Center.

May provide meals, trips, educational courses, art classes, self-defense classes and other social functions

Shepherd's Centers of America
1-816-523-1080: 6700 Troost, Suite 616, Kansas City, MO 64131

Provides information regarding interfaith ministry programs which provide home-care services

Social Security Administration
1-800-772-1213: 6401 Security Blvd., Room 4J5, West High Rise, Baltimore, MD 21235

Provides free information and free publications: Understanding Social Security; Hospice Benefits; and Medicare and Coordinated Plans. Provides income after age 65, or if you become severely disabled, also provides income to surviving spouse and dependent children, should death occur; information on insurance benefits and future SS earnings Direct Deposit of your Social Security check is a great way to prevent mail theft, having to balance extra finances and making unnecessary trips to the bank.

SSI-Supplemental Security Income
1-800-772-1213, TDD 1-800-955-8771 (allows calls to be placed between TDD users and non-users): Assures a minimum level of income. If you qualify for SSI you automatically are eligible for Medicaid. Your state HRS determines eligibility for Medicaid

Stamps By Mail
1-800-782-6724: United States Post Office

United Seniors Health Cooperative
1-202-393-6222: 1331 H St. NW, Suite 500, Washington, DC 20005-4706

Provides information, referrals and publications

VNAA — Visiting Nurse Associations of America
1-800-426-2547: 3801 East Florida Ave., Suite 900, Denver, CO 80210

Provides representation for about 500 skilled-nursing associations

Volunteers of America, Inc.
1-800-899-0089: 3939 N. Causeway Blvd., Suite 400, Metairie, LA 70002-1777
Provides information regarding housing, home improvements, and assisted living

Well Spouse Foundation
1-212-644-1241: P.O. Box 801, New York, NY 10023
Provides information; support; and referrals to support groups for individuals caring for a sick spouse. Also provides a bi-monthly newsletter.

Widowed Persons Service
1-202-434-2260: 601 E Street NW, Washington, DC 20049
Provides support services through AARP

GRIEF AND BEREAVEMENT

Center for Loss and Life Transition
1-970-226-6050: 3735 Broken Bow Rd., Fort Collins, CO 80526
Provides information and local referrals for bereavement support

Choice in Dying
1-800-989-9455: 200 Varick St., New York, NY 10014
Provides information; counseling; and state-specific advance directives

Compassionate Friends Hotline
1-708-990-0010: P.O. Box 3696, Oakbrook, IL 60522-3696
Provides referrals to local support groups

Funeral and Memorial Societies of America
1-800-765-0107: 6900 Lost Lake Rd., Egg Harbor, WI 54209
Provides information and guidance

Grief Recovery Institute
1-213-650-1234: 8306 Wilshire Blvd., Suite 21A, Beverly Hills, CA 90211
Provides information regarding bereavement support groups

National Catholic Ministry to the Bereaved
1-216-441-2125: 9412 Heath Ave., Cleveland, OH 44102
Provides local referrals and support

National Funeral Directors Association
1-800- 228-6332: 11121 West Oklahoma Ave., Milwaukee, WI 53227
Provides local referrals to funeral directors and guidance for burials and memorial services

National Funeral Directors' Service Consumer Arbitration Program
1-414-541-2500: P.O. Box 27641, Milwaukee, WI 53227-0641
Provides arbitration for problems with funeral directors

National Right to Life Committee
1-202-626-8800: 419 Seventh St. NW, Suite 500, Washington, DC 20004
Provides information opposing euthanasia; a state-specific Will To Live; and guidance for treatments refused by doctors and/or hospitals

HEARING/SPEECH IMPAIRED

American Academy of Otolaryngology—Head and Neck Surgery
1-703-836-4444: 1 Prince Street, Alexandria, VA 22314
Provides information and local referrals. A professional association

American Hearing Research Foundation
1-312-726-9670: 55 East Washington Street, Chicago, IL 60602
Provides information and local referrals

American Speech-Language Hearing Association

1-800-638-8255 or 1-301-897-8682: 10801 Rockville Pike, Rockville, MD 20852

Provides information and referrals. A membership organization for audiologists and speech pathologists

American Tinnitus Association

1-503-248-9985: P.O. Box 5, Portland, OR 97207

Provides information; referrals to local support groups; and publications including a newsletter regarding tinnitus (ringing in the ears)

Association of Late-Deafened Adults

1-708-445-0860 (TDD or fax only): P.O. Box 930075, Rochester, NY 14692-7375

Provides information, a newsletter, and sponsors. A membership organization

AT&T Accessible Communication Product Center

1-800-233-1222: 5 Wood Hollow Road, Room 1119, Parsippany, NJ 07054

Provides information and a catalogue of equipment for the hearing/speech impaired

Better Hearing Institute—Hearing Helpline

1-800-327-9355: P.O. Box 1840, Washington, DC 20013

Provides educational information and publications. A non-profit organization

Hearing Aid Helpline

1-800-521-5247: 20361 Middlebelt Road, Livonia, MI 48152

Provides information and local referrals regarding hearing aids

Hear Now

1-800-648-4327: 9745 East Hampden Ave., Suite 300, Denver, CO 80231

Provides hearing aids and cochlear implants free to low-income individuals. A private, non-profit organization

Modern Talking Picture Service Caption Films and Videos

1-800-237-6213: 5000 Park St. North, St. Petersburg, FL 33709

Provides videos with captioning free of charge. Sponsored by the U.S. Dept. of Education

National Aphasia Association

1-800-922-4622: P.O. Box 1887, New York, NY 10156

Provides information; local referrals to services and support groups; and public awareness promotions

National Association of the Deaf

1-301-587-1788 or 1-301-587-1789 (TDD): 814 Thayer Ave., Silver Springs, MD 20910

Provides information; advocacy; volunteer programs; legal services; scholarships; and teacher certification. A membership organization

National Information Center on Deafness

1-202-651-5051: 800 Florida Ave. NE, Washington, DC 20002

Provides information services; referrals; legal services; and publications regarding all aspects of deafness, discrimination and violation of civil rights complaints

National Institute on Deafness and Other Communication Disorders

1-800-241-1044: Information Clearinghouse, 1 Communication Ave., Bethesda, MD 20892

Provides information and publications regarding hearing, language and balance

Self-Help for Hard-of Hearing People

1-301-657-2248 or 1-657-2249 (TDD): 7910 Woodmont Ave., Suite 1200, Bethesda, MD 20814

Provides information; local referrals; and a bi-monthly journal

HISPANIC SERVICES

Asociacion Nacional Pro Personal Mayores (National Association for Hispanic Elderly)
1-213-487-1922: 3325 Wilshire Blvd., Suite 800, Los Angeles, CA 90010-1784
Provides publications and referral services

National Association for Hispanic Elderly
1-213-487-1922: 3325 Wilshire Blvd., Suite 800, Los Angeles, CA 90010-1784
Provides information; advocacy; and publications in Spanish and English

National Hispanic Council on Aging
1-202-265-1288: 2713 Ontario Rd. NW, Suite 200, Washington, DC 20009
Provides advocacy, information and publications: The Hispanic Elderly: A Cultural Signature ($18.00); Elderly Latinos: Issues and Solutions for the 21st Century ($20.45); Empowering Hispanic Families: Critical Issues for the 90's ($20.45)

HOME CARE

American Association of Continuity of Care
1-203-586-7525: 638 Prospect Ave., Hartford, CT 06105-4298
Provides standards for home care

National Association for Home Care
1-202-547-7424: 519 C St. NE, Washington, DC 20002
Provides local referrals to home health agencies, and a free publication: What is Home Care?

VNAA — Visiting Nurse Associations of America
1-800-426-2547: 3801 East Florida Ave., Suite 900, Denver, CO 80210
Provides representation for about 500 skilled-nursing associations

HOSPICE

Family Resource Service
1-800-847-5437: 1400 Union Meeting Rd., Suite 102, Blue Bell, PA 19422
Provides information regarding respite services, home-healthcare, and support groups

Foundation for Hospice and Homecare
1-202-547-6586: 320 A Street NE, Washington, DC 20002
Provides information and a free publication: All About Hospice

Hospice Association of America
1-202-546-4759: 519 C St. NE, Washington, DC 20002
Provides publications about hospice services

Hospice Education Institute
1-800-331-1620: Hospice Link, 190 W. Brooke Rd., Essex, CT 06426
Provides information; local referrals; and publications

National Hospice Organization—Hospice Helpline
1-800-658-8898 or 1-703-243-5900:
1901 N. Monroe St. Suite 901, Arlington, VA 22209
Provides comprehensive emotional, spiritual, physical and social services to terminally ill patients and their families; compassionate care for patients; information; and publications. Hospice Helpline provides local referrals

INCONTINENCE

American Foundation for Urologic Disease
1-800-242-2383: 300 West Pratt Street, Suite 401, Baltimore, MD 21201

Provides educational information regarding urinary tract, rectal, and prostate diseases and disorders

HIP—Help for Incontinent People
1-800-252-3337 or 1-803-579-7900: P.O. Box 8310, Spartanburg, SC 29305

Provides publications; audio-visuals; Resource Guide; and local support group referrals

International Foundation for Bowel Dysfunction
1-414-241-9479: P.O. Box 17864, Milwaukee, WI 53217

Provides free information and publications regarding all aspects of bowel diseases and disorders

National Kidney and Urologic Diseases Information Clearinghouse
1-301-654-4415: 3 Information Way, Bethesda, MD 20892

Provides free information and publications regarding all aspects of kidney, prostate, and urinary tract diseases and disorders

Simon Foundation for Incontinence
1-800-23-SIMON or 1-708-864-3913: P.O. Box 815, Wilmette, IL 60091

Provides a 24-hour hotline; and educational information including: video and audio tapes, articles, and a newsletters

INSURANCE: HEALTH AND LONG-TERM CARE (SUPPLEMENTAL)

Center for Medicare Advocacy
1-800-262-4414: P.O. Box 350, Willimantic, CT 06226

Provides free legal help to Connecticut residents; information and local referrals to residents of other state

Connecticut Partnership for Long-term Care
1-800-547-3443 (Connecticut residents) or 1-203-418-6318 (out of state residents): Office of Policy & Management, 80 Washington St., Hartford, CT 06106-4459

Provides information regarding Medicare and private insurance companies offering long-term care policies and asset protection

Indiana Long-term Care Program
1-800-452-4800 (Indiana residents) or 1-317-232-2187 (out of state residents): 402 W. Washington St., W353, Indianapolis, IN 46204

Provides information regarding Medicare and private insurance companies offering long-term care policies and asset protection

GHI-Group Health Incorporated
1-800-223-9870: P.O. Box 1701, New York, NY 10023

Coordinates healthcare services

GHPs -Group Health Plans
1-800-999-1118

Provides healthcare for Medicare beneficiaries with permanent kidney failure and/or certain other disabilities, or those who continue to work beyond age 65

Health Insurance Association of America
1-800-635-1271: Consumer Information Services, 555 13th Street NW, Suite 600 East, Washington, DC 20004-1109

Provides information, a list of companies that offer long-term care insurance, and a free publication: Guide to Long-term Care Insurance

Health Insurance Counseling and Advocacy Program
Contact your State Insurance Division-Consumer Affairs, or State Office on Aging.
These numbers are normally listed under *State* or *Government* in your telephone directory.
Provides information and advocacy

HMOs—Health Management Organization
Contact your state insurance counselor or Health Care Financing Administration
1-800-772-1213 or 1-202-619-0100: U.S. Dept. of Health and Human Services,
200 Independence Ave. SW, Washington, DC 20201
Provides alternatives to health insurance

Medicare Hotline
1-800-638-6833 or 1-800-492-6603 (Maryland):
Provides free information; answers questions; reports Medicare fraud

National Association of Claims
1-800-660-0665: Assistance Professionals, 5329 South Main St.,
Downers Grove, IL 60515
Provides representation for medical claims agents; consumer publications; and makes
local referrals. A professional association

National Association of Insurance Commissioners
1-816-842-3600: 120 W. 12th St., Suite 1100, Kansas City, MO 64105
Provides information and a free publication: A Shopper's Guide to Long-term Care
Insurance

National Consumers League
1-202-835-3323: 1701 K Street NW, Washington, DC 20006
Provides free consumer publications and information on Medicare, Medicaid,
financial issues and medications

National Flood Insurance Program
1-800-638-6620: P.O. Box 6464, Rockville, MD 20849-6464
Processes applications

National Health Information Center
1-800-336-4797: P.O. Box 1133, Washington, DC 20013
Provides information and local referrals regarding health and health insurance.
Sponsored by the Department of Health and Human Services

National Insurance Consumers Helpline
1-800-942-4242: 555 13th St. NW, Washington, DC 20004-1109
Provides referrals and information regarding Medicare, long-term care and health,
life, home auto and business insurance

United Seniors Health Cooperative
1-202-393-6222: 1331 H St. NW, Suite 500, Washington, DC 20005-4706
Provides information regarding insurance; and referrals and publications designed to aid
the elderly in leading healthy, independent lives. A non-profit organization

LEGAL

ABA — American Bar Association
1-800-621-6159: 750 N. Lakeshore Dr., Chicago, IL 60611
Provides legal publications for the aged, and local referrals

Commission on Legal Problems of the Elderly—American Bar Association
1-202-662-8690: 1800 M Street NW, South Lobby, Washington, DC 20036
Provides consumer information and publications; technical resources for lawyers; and
local referrals for legal aid

Health Care Financing Administration
1-800-772-1213 or 1-202-619-0100: U.S. Dept. of Health and Human Services,
200 Independence Ave. SW., Washington, DC 20201
Provides information and free publications: <u>Guide to Health Insurance for People With Medicare</u>; <u>Medicare and Advance Directives</u>; and <u>Medicare Handbook 1996</u>

IRS-Internal Revenue Service
1-800-829-1040
Provides information regarding Federal Income Tax

Legal Counsel for the Elderly—American Association of Retired Persons
1-800-424-3410: 601 E Street NW, Washington, DC 20049
Provides hotlines; free legal advice; and local referrals to low-cost legal help

National Academy of Elder Law Attorneys, Inc.
1-520-881-4005: 1604 N. Country Club Rd., Tucson, AZ 85716
Provides local referrals, and free publication: <u>Questions & Answers When Looking for an Elder Law Attorney</u>

National Clearing House for Legal Services, Inc.
1-312-263-3830: 205 W. Monroe St., Second Floor, Chicago, IL 60606-5013
Provides publications on health, senior citizens, and housing

National Organization of Social Security Claimants Representatives
1-914-735-8812: 9 East Central Ave., Pearl River, NJ 10965
Provides attorneys who specialize in Social Security law appeals and Supplemental Security Insurance (SSI)

National Senior Citizens Law Center
1-202-887-5280: 1815 H St. NW, Suite 700, Washington, DC 20006
Provides free publications catalogue

NOLO Press
1-800-336-4797: 950 Parker St., Berkeley, CA 94710-9867
Provides information, books and software regarding estate planning; wills; nursing homes; and long-term care insurance

Social Security Administration
1-800-772-1213: 6401 Security Blvd., Room 4J5, West High Rise, Baltimore, MD 21235
Provides free information and free publications: <u>Understanding Social Security</u>; <u>Hospice Benefits</u>; and <u>Medicare and Coordinated Plans</u>

LIVING ARRANGEMENTS AND HOUSING

Aging Network Services
1-301-657-4329 4400: East West Hwy., Suite 907, Bethesda, MD 20814
Provides social work services for elderly and families. National service consisting of screened and licensed counselors. Half-hour, free, in-home visit, then assessment and referrals to local resources will be made

American Association of Homes and Services for the Aging
1-202-783-2242: 901 E Street NW, Suite 500, Washington, DC 20004
Provides information; consumer publications regarding housing and services including: <u>Consumer's Directory of Continuing Care Retirement Communities</u>, $24.95; and a list of continuing care retirement communities

American Health Care Association
1-800-321-0343 or 1-202-842-4444: 1201 L Street NW, Washington, DC 20005
Provides publications regarding nursing homes

Assisted Living Facilities Association of America
1-703-691-8100: 9411 Lee Highway, Plaza Suite J, Fairfax, VA 22031
Provides information and publications regarding choosing assisted living

California Advocates for Nursing Home Reform
1-415-474-5171: 1610 Bush Street, San Francisco, CA 94109
Provides advocacy for nursing homes

Concerned Relatives of Nursing Home Patients
1-216-321-0403: P.O. Box 18820, Cleveland Heights, OH 44118-8820
Provides information regarding nursing home placement, Medicare and Medicaid

Continuing Care Accreditation Commission
1-203-418-6318:
Office of Policy and Management, 80 Washington St., Hartford, CT 06106-4459
Provides information regarding accredited continuing care retirement communities

Council of Better Business Bureaus, Inc.
1-703-276-0100: Publications Dept., 4200 Wilson Blvd., Suite 800,
Arlington, VA 22203
Provides information regarding long-term nursing home care; Continuing Care
Retirement Communities; Medicare and Medigap

Kelly Assisted Living
1-800-937-5355 or consult your local telephone directory:
Provides information packages on local service providers; in-home companionship
and care to individuals who need assistance with daily living activities for short- and
long-term disabilities (surgery recovery, Alzheimer's, etc.)

Local Elder Care Services
Contact your local elder care agency
May provide adult day care; respite relief and care services; companion services; tele-
phone reassurance; home maintenance; lawn care; house cleaning; grocery shopping
assistance; transportation; Adopt-A-Grandparent Program; Senior Work Program; Foster
Grandparent Program

National Citizens Coalition for Nursing Home Reform
1-202-332-2275: 1424 16th St. NW, Suite 202, Washington, DC 20036-2211
Consumer advocacy, local referrals, publication of consumer guidelines

NAAA-National Association of Area Agencies on Aging
1-800-677-1116 or 1-202-296-8130; FAX: 1- 202-296-8134:
1112 16th St. NW, Suite 100, Washington, DC 20036
Provides local elder care locator service; and local referrals. A non-profit organization

National Association for Home Care
1-202-547-7472: 519 C St. NE, Washington, DC 20002
Provides information and publications regarding choosing home-healthcare

National Association of Professional Geriatric Care Managers
1-520-881-8008: 1604 North Country Club Road, Tucson, AZ 85716
Provides referrals to care managers. Membership trade organization

National Association of Social Workers
1-800-638-8799 (Ext. 291): 750 First St. NE, Washington, DC 20002
Provides local referrals. Trade association for social workers

National Citizens' Coalition for Nursing Home Reform
1-202-332-2275: 1424 16th Street NW, Suite 202, Washington, DC 20036
Provides information; advocacy; ombudsman programs; guidance in selecting a nursing
home; and local referrals

National Council on the Aging

1-202-479-1200: 409 Third Street SW, Washington, DC 20024

Provides information; creates programs; trains professionals and volunteers; advocacy; local referrals; publications; and services regarding legal, financial, social, nutrition, health, living arrangements, respite care, and support groups. A private, non-profit organization Membership required

National Council of Senior Citizens

1-202-624-9340 or 1-202-347-8800: 1331 F St. NW, Suite 800, Washington, DC 20004-1171

Provides nursing home information; locator service; advocacy; two publications: Bill of Rights; and Coping With Aging; advocacy; and membership benefits: insurance, prescription medications, and travel services. A membership organization.

National Eldercare Institute on Housing

1-213-740-1364: Andrus Gerontology Center, University of Southern California, Los Angeles, CA 90089-0191

Provides information regarding housing alternatives

National Family Caregivers Association

1-800-896-3650: 9223 Longbranch Parkway, Silver Springs, MD 20901-3642

Provides information and quarterly publication: Take Care! Membership required

National Federation of Interfaith Volunteer Caregivers

1-800-350-7438: 368 Broadway, Suite 103, Kingston, NY 12401

Provides non-profit volunteers who offer in-home care, companionship and assistance

National Institute on Aging Information Center

1-800-222-2225: P.O. Box 8057, Gaithersburg, MD 20898-8057

Provides several free publications, including a resource directory for elderly and a resource directory for women's health issues. Also distributes Ages Pages

National Shared Housing Resource Center

1-410-235-4454: 321 East 25th St., Baltimore, MD 21218

Provides information and local referrals designed to bring roommates together

Nursing Home Information Service — National Council of Senior Citizens

1-202-347-8800 (ext 340/341): 1331 F Street NW, Washington, DC 20004

Provides information on adult day-care, long-term care and home-healthcare.

MEALS AND NUTRITION

Food Stamp Program

Consult your local telephone directory or call Social Security at 1-800-772-1213:

Provides supplemental income for nutritional needs: State HRS may offer this assistance

National Association of Meal Programs

1-703-548-5558: 101 North Alfred Street, Suite 202, Alexandria, VA 22314

Provides information for providers and local referrals for community dining and in-home meal services. A membership organization

National Meals on Wheels Foundation

1-800-999-6262 or 1-616-531-9909: 2675 44th St. SW, Suite 305, Grand Rapids, MI 49509

Provides grants to meal programs; meal delivery; volunteer referrals and service hotline

National Safety Council

1-800-621-7619 or 1-312-527-4800: 1121 Spring Lake Dr., Itasca, IL 60143

Provides information on health and safety

Nutrition Hotline — American Dietetic Association
1-800-366-1655: 216 West Jackson Blvd., Suite 800, Chicago, IL 60606
Provides nutrition information and referrals to a local dietician

MEDICAL

ALZHEIMER'S DISEASE; OTHER DEMENTIAS AND MEMORY LOSS

Alzheimer's Association
1-800-272-3900: 919 N. Michigan Ave., Suite 1000, Chicago, IL 60611
Provides nationwide referrals to local chapters, services and support groups

Alzheimer's Disease Education and Referral Center
1-800-438-4390: P.O. Box 8250, Silver Springs, MD 20907
Provides free information on Alzheimer's and other dementia related diseases

American Occupational Therapy Association
1-301-652-2628: P.O. Box 31220, 4720 Montgomery Drive, Bethesda, MD 20824
Provides consumer information and publications regarding Alzheimer's disease, living
with a disability, recovery and home modifications

Family Caregiver Alliance
1-800-445-8106 or 1-415-434-3388:
425 Bush Street, Suite 500, San Francisco, CA 94018
Provides information regarding memory loss and brain injury

ARTHRITIS

Arthritis Foundation
1-800-283-7800 or 1-404-872-7100: 1130 West Peachtree St., Atlanta, GA 30309
Assistance for those diagnosed with arthritis
Provides free brochures; bulletins; referrals to local foundation for support groups,
exercise classes, and a list of doctors; and funds research

Arthritis Foundation
1-800-283-7800: Information Line, P.O. Box 19000, Atlanta, GA 30326
Provides information and nationwide referrals to local chapters and support groups

National Arthritis and Musculoskeletal and Skin Diseases
1-301- 495- 4484: Information Clearinghouse, 1 AMS Circle, Bethesda, MD 20892
Provides information and free publications regarding diseases of the joints, bones and skir

National Osteoporosis Foundation
1-800-223-9994 or 1-202-223-2226: 1150 17th St. NW, Suite 500, Washington, DC
20036
Provides free information and reports

CANCER

American Cancer Society
1-800-227-2345 or 1-404-320-3333: 1599 Clifton Rd. NE, Atlanta, GA 30329
Provides free information; answers personal questions; publications; and referrals

American Cancer Society Hotline
1-800-ACS-2345 or 1-415-394-7100:
235 Montgomery Street, Suite 320, San Francisco, CA 94104
Provides local referrals

Cancer Information Service
1-800-422-6237 (1-800-4-CANCER)
National Cancer Institute, Building 31, Room 10A24, Bethesda, MD 20892
Provides free information; referrals to local centers and support groups; and publications

National Coalition for Cancer Survivorship
1-301-650-8868: 1010 Wayne Ave., Silver Springs, MD 20910
Provides free information and local referrals

DENTAL

National Institute of Dental Research
1-301-496-4261: 9000 Rockville Pike, Bethesda, MD 20892
Offers free information on dentistry and periodontal care

DIABETES

American Association of Diabetes Educators
1-800-338-3633: 444 N. Michigan Ave., Suite 1240, Chicago, IL 60611
Provides local referrals to diabetes educators. A professional association for diabetes educators

American Diabetes Association
1-800-868-7888: 1660 Duke Street, Alexandria, VA 22314
Provides free information and local referrals

National Diabetes Information Clearinghouse
1-301-654-3327: 1 Information Way, Bethesda, MD 20892
Provides free information and publications

FOOT DISORDERS

American Podiatric Medical Association
1-800-366-8227: 9312 Old Georgetown Rd., Bethesda, MD 20814
Provides information and publications regarding foot care and diseases; and referrals

HEART

American Heart Association National Center and Stroke Connection
1-800-242-8721 or 1-800-553-6321 or 1-214-373-6300:
7272 Greenville Ave., Dallas, TX 65231-4596
Provides free publications

American Medical Association
1-312-464-5000: 515 N. State St., Chicago, IL 60610
Provides local referrals

American Physical Therapy Association
1-703-684-2782: 1111 North Fairfax St., Alexandria, VA 22314
Provides information; publications; and local referrals

National Heart, Lung, and Blood Institute Information Center
1-301-251-1222: P.O. Box 30105, Bethesda, MD 20824
Provides information and publications

HUNTINGTON'S DISEASE

Huntington's Disease
1-800-345-HDSA or 1-212 242-1968:
140 W. 22nd Street, Sixth Floor, New York, NY 10011-2420
Provides publications; audio-visuals; nationwide chapters; and local referrals

MEDICINES AND MISCELLANEOUS HEALTH ISSUES

Council on Family Health
1-212-598-3617: 225 Park Ave. South, Suite 1700, New York, NY 10003
Provides information regarding medicines and drug interactions for elderly persons

Family Caregiver Project
1-704-547-4758: University of North Carolina, Charlotte;
Dept. of Psychology, Charlotte, NC 28223
Provides manuals on caregiving and particular illnesses, and a publication: <u>Caring Families</u>

National Digestive Diseases Information Clearinghouse
1-800-891-5389 or 1-301-654-3810: 2 Information Way, Bethesda, MD 20892
Provides free information and publications

National Health Information Center
1-800-336-4797: U.S. Dept. of Health and Human Services, P.O. Box 1133,
Washington, DC 20013-1133
Provides information; toll-free health lines; publications for particular diseases; and local referrals regarding health and health insurance. Sponsored by the Department of Health and Human Services

National Institute of Health
1-301-496-4000: 9000 Rockville Pike, Bethesda, MD 20892
Provides several publications on particular diseases, health, and aging. Publishes:
<u>Ages Pages</u>

National Organization for Rare Disorders
1-800-999-6673: P.O. Box 8923, New Fairfield, CT 06812
Provides information and local referrals. First request is free. A non-profit clearinghouse

National Osteoporosis Foundation
1-800-223-9994 or 1-202-223-2226: 1150 17th St. NW, Suite 500, Washington, DC 20036
Provides free information and reports

National Rural Health Association
1-816-756-3140: 301 E. Armour Blvd., Suite 420, Kansas City, MO 64111
Provides information, resources and publications

National Safety Council
1-800-621-7619 or 1-312-527-4800: 1121 Spring Lake Dr., Itasca, IL 60143
Provides information on health and safety

Office of Disease Prevention and Health Promotion
1-800-336-4797, U.S. Dept. of Health and Human Services Information Center
Provides health information and referrals (English and Spanish)

United Seniors Health Cooperative
1-202-393-6222: 1331 H St. NW, Suite 500, Washington, DC 20005-4706
Provides information, referrals and publications designed to aid the elderly in leading healthy, independent lives. A non-profit organization

MENTAL HEALTH: PSYCHOLOGICAL AND PSYCHIATRIC SERVICES

AAMFT — American Association for Marriage and Family Therapy
1-800-374-2638: 1100 17th Street NW, 10th Floor, Washington, DC 20036
Provides local referrals for issues pertaining to the elderly and their families

American Psychiatric Association
1-202-682-6000: 1400 K Street NW, Washington, DC 20005
Provides free publications regarding mental disorders of the aged

American Psychological Association
1-800-374-2721: 750 First Street NE, Washington, DC 20002-4242
Provides information and referrals

American Self-Help Clearinghouse
1-201-625-7101: 25 Pocono Road, St. Clare's-Riverside Medical Center, Denville, NJ 07834
Provides information and referrals

NAMI — National Alliance for the Mentally Ill
1-800-950-6264 or 1-703-524-7600: 200 N. Glene Road, Suite 1015, Arlington, VA 22201
Provides consumer information and referrals to local services and support groups

National Association of Social Workers
1-202-408-8600: 750 First Street NE, Washington, DC 20002
Provides information and referrals to local services, therapists and support groups

National Foundation for Depressive Illness
1-800-248-4381: P.O. Box 2257, New York, NY 10116
Provides information; publications and referrals to local specialists

NIMH — National Institute of Mental Health
1-301-443-4513 or 1-800-421-4211 for DART (Depression Awareness,
Recognition and Treatment Public Inquiries Office, Room 7C-O2, 5600 Fishers Lane, Rockville, MD 20857
Provides information; publications; and local referrals to specialists

National Mental Health Association
1-800-969-6642: 1021 Prince Street, Alexandria, VA 22314
Provides information and local referrals

National Self-Help Clearinghouse
1-212-354-8525: 25 West 43rd Street, Room 620, New York, NY 10036
Provides consumer information; local referrals; and information on starting support groups

PARKINSON'S DISEASE
American Parkinson's Disease Association
1-800-223-2732: 60 Bay Street, Room 401, Staten Island, NY 10301
Provides information; publications; and local referrals

National Institute of Neurological Disorders and Stroke
1-800-352-9424: Information Office, Building 31, Room 8A16, 31 Center Dr., MSC2540, Bethesda, MD 20892
Provides nationwide referrals to local centers and information on Alzheimer's, epilepsy, Parkinson's, stroke and other brain-related disorders

National Parkinson's Foundation
1-900-327-4545: 1501 NW 9th Ave., Miami, FL 33136
Provides information and local referrals to specialists

Parkinson's Disease Foundation
1-800-457-6676: William Black Medical Research Building,
Columbia Presbyterian Medical Center, 650 W. 168th St., New York, NY 10032
Provides educational information; support group referral by zip code; and sponsors research

RESPIRATORY AND LUNG DISEASES
American Lung Association
1-800-586-4872: G.P.O. Box 596, New York, NY 10016
Provides information on all aspects of lung diseases and local referrals for medical care, smoking cessation, and support groups

SKIN DISORDERS

American Academy of Dermatology
P.O. Box 681069, Schaumburg, IL 60168
Provides free publications when requests are accompanied by a self-addressed, stamped envelope

National Arthritis and Musculoskeletal and Skin Diseases
1-301- 495- 4484: Information Clearinghouse, 1 AMS Circle, Bethesda, MD 20892
Provides information and free publications regarding diseases of the joints, bones and skin

STROKE

American Heart Association National Center and Stroke Connection
1-800-242-8721 or 1-800-553-6321 or 1-214-373-6300
7272 Greenville Ave., Dallas, TX 65231-4596
Provides free publications

American Physical Therapy Association
1-703-684-2782: 1111 North Fairfax St., Alexandria, VA 22314
Provides information; publications; and local referrals

American Speech-Language Hearing Association
1-800-638-8255 or 1-301-897-8682: 10801 Rockville Pike, Rockville, MD 20852
Provides information and referrals. A membership organization for audiologists and speech pathologists

Courage Stroke Network
1-800-553-6321 or 1-612-588-0811: 3915 Golden Valley Rd., Golden Valley, MN 55422
Provides information and products pertaining to stroke victims

Family Caregiver Alliance
1-415-434-3388: 425 Bush Street, Suite 500, San Francisco, CA 94108
Provides information and referrals

National Aphasia Association
1-800-922-4622: P.O. Box 1887, New York, NY 10156
Provides information; local referrals to services and support groups; and public awareness promotions

National Institute of Neurological Disorders and Stroke
1-800-352-9424: Information Office, Building 31, Room 8A16, 31 Center Dr., MSC2540, Bethesda, MD 20892
Provides nationwide referrals to local centers and information on Alzheimer's, epilepsy, Parkinson's, stroke and other brain related disorders

National Stroke Association
1-800-787-6537: 8480 East Orchard Road, Suite 1000, Englewood, CO 80111
Provides information and local referrals to specialists, support groups, rehabilitation centers and services

MEDICARE and MEDICAID

Concerned Relatives of Nursing Home Patients
1-216-321-0403: P.O. Box 18820, Cleveland Heights, OH 44118-8820
Provides information regarding nursing home placement, Medicare and Medicaid

Connecticut Partnership for Long-term Care
1-203-418-6318 or 1-800-547-3443 (Connecticut residents):
Office of Policy & Management, 80 Washington St., Hartford, CT 06106-4459
Provides information regarding Medicare and private insurance companies offering
long-term care policies and asset protection

Council of Better Business Bureaus, Inc.
1-703-276-0100: Publications Dept., 4200 Wilson Blvd., Suite 800, Arlington, VA 22203
Provides information regarding long-term nursing home care; Continuing Care Retirement
Communities; Medicare and Medigap

Health Care Financing Administration
1-800-772-1213 or 1-202-619-0100: U.S. Dept. of Health and Human Services,
200 Independence Ave. SW, Washington, DC 20201
Provides free publications: Medicare Handbook 1996; Guide to Health Insurance for
People with Medicare; and Medicare and Advance Directives

Indiana Long-term Care Program
1-800-452-4800 (Indiana residents) or 1-317-232-2187 (out of state residents):
402 W. Washington St., W353, Indianapolis, IN 46204
Provides information regarding Medicare and private insurance companies
offering long-term care policies and asset protection

Medicare Data-match Center
1-800-999-1118: P.O. Box 1811, New York, NY 10023-1479
Identifies cases for Medicare eligibility. Provides healthcare for Medicare
beneficiaries with permanent kidney failure and/or certain other disabilities or
those who continue working past age 65

Medicare Insurance Help Line
1-800-772-1213
Provides information regarding Medicare

New York State Partnership for Long-term Care
1-518-473-7705 (New York residents only): NYS DSS, 40 N. Pearl St., Albany, NY 12243
Provides information regarding Medicaid and private insurance companies offering
long-term care policies and asset protection.

Social Security Administration
1-800-772-1213: 6401 Security Blvd., Room 4J5, West High Rise, Baltimore, MD 21235
Provides free information and free publications: Understanding Social Security;
Hospice Benefits; and Medicare and Coordinated Plans

MILITARY-RELATED SERVICES

Blinded Veterans Association
1-202-371-8880: 477 H Street NW, Washington, DC 20001
Provides assistance for obtaining benefits, rehabilitation, and services

Department of Defense
1-314-263-3901: National Personnel Record Center, 9700 Page Blvd., St. Louis, MO 63132
Provides copies of military discharge certificates

Paralyzed Veterans of America
1-800-424-8200: 801 18th Street NW, Washington, DC 20006
Provides information on benefits, home modifications, and adjusting to and living with a
disability; and local referrals

VA-Department of Veterans Affairs
1-800-827-1000: Secretary of Veterans Affairs, Mr. Jesse Brown, 810 Vermont Ave NW, Washington, DC 20420
Provides benefits for qualified veterans

MISCELLANEOUS INFORMATION

Clothing- Local Red Cross, Salvation Army, Goodwill Industries
Some local grocery stores deliver
Some local pharmacies deliver

OLDER WOMEN'S ISSUES

National Institute on Aging Information Center
1-800-222-2225: P.O. Box 8057, Gaithersburg, MD 20898-8057
Provides several free publications including a resource directory for elderly health issues and a resource directory for women's health issues. Also distributes Ages Pages

Older Women's League
1-800-825-3695 or 1-202-783-6686: 666 11th St. NW, Suite 700, Washington, DC 20001
Provides information and publications regarding older women and pensions, and legal issues; caregiving; poverty; housing; and long-term care

People's Medical Society
1-610-770-1670: 14 East Minor Street, Emmaus, PA 18049
Provides information and advocacy for patient's rights and family rights; monitors the practices of medical professionals and organizations; provisions for filing complaints

PHYSICAL FITNESS FOR THE ELDERLY

American Alliance for Health, Physical Education, Recreation and Dance
1-800-321-0789: P.O. Box 385, Oxon Hill, MD 20750
Provides (for-sale) publications on exercise for the elderly and disabled

American Physical Therapy Association
1-703-684-2782: 1111 North Fairfax St., Alexandria, VA 22314
Provides information; publications; and local referrals

Arthritis Foundation
1-800-283-7800: Information Line, P.O. Box 19000, Atlanta, GA 30326
Provides information on exercise and referrals to local chapters and exercise classes

President's Council on Physical Fitness and Sports
1-202-272-3421: 701 Pennsylvania Ave. NW, Room 250, Washington, DC 20034
Provides information and a free publication: Nolan Ryan Fitness Guide, for people over 40. To order: Nolan Ryan Fitness Guide, P.O. Box 22091, Albany, NY 12201-2091

VISION IMPAIRMENT AND SERVICES FOR THE BLIND

American Council of the Blind
1-800-424-8666 or 1-202-467-5081: 1155 15th Street NW, Suite 720, Washington, DC 20005
Provides information, advocacy and local referrals for services and equipment

American Foundation for the Blind
1-800-232-5463: 11 Penn Plaza, New York, NY 10001
Provides information and local referrals to state agencies, rehabilitation centers, and low-cost vision centers

Association for Macular Diseases
1-212-605-3719: 210 East 64th Street, New York, NY 10021
Provides information, local referrals and emotional support. A volunteer organization

Better Vision Institute
1-800-424-8422: 1800 North Kent Street, Suite 904, Rosslyn, VA 22209
Provides educational information regarding eye diseases and aging

Blinded Veterans Association
1-202-371-8880: 477 H Street NW, Washington, DC 20001
Provides assistance for obtaining benefits, rehabilitation, and services

Glaucoma Research Foundation
1-800-826-6693: 490 Post Street, Suite 830, San Francisco, CA 94102
Provides a self-help hotline, information, local referrals to specialists; publications including: Understanding and Living with Glaucoma, and a newsletter

The Lighthouse National Center for Vision and Aging
1-800-334-5497 or 1-800-0077 or 1-212-821-9200: 800 Second Ave.,
New York, NY 10017
Provides information regarding every aspect of eye diseases and vision loss; local referrals to state agencies and support groups

National Association for the Visually Handicapped
1-212-889-3141: 22 West 21st Street, New York, NY 10010
Provides information regarding all aspects of eye diseases, emotional issues of vision loss, and referrals to local specialists and clinics. Also provides a lending library of large-print books and a catalogue of visual aids

National Eye Care Project—American Academy of Ophthalmology
1-800-222-3937: P.O. Box 7424, San Francisco, CA 94120
Provides information on eye diseases and local referrals to low-cost services

National Eye Institute Information Office
1-301-496-5248: 31 Center Drive, MSC2510, Building 31, Room 6A32,
Bethesda, MD 20892
Provides information and publications on the latest research and treatments

National Federation of the Blind
1-410-659-9314: 1800 Johnson Street, Baltimore, MD 21230
Provides information and programs including medical, social, legal and emotional issues of the blind and makes referrals to local support groups and services

National Library Service for the Blind and Physically Handicapped
1-800-424-8567: Library of Congress, 1291 Taylor Street NW, Washington, DC 20542
Provides free information; Loans playing equipment and books on tapes, disk and in Braille. Free

Prevent Blindness America (National Center for Sight)
41-800-331-2020: 500 East Remington Road, Schaumburg, IL 60173
Provides information and local referrals to support groups

INDEX

PERSONAL REFERENCE